TEILHARD'S
VISION OF
THE PAST

TEILHARD'S VISION OF THE PAST

The Making of a Method

ROBERT J. O'CONNELL, S.J.

1907

New York
FORDHAM UNIVERSITY PRESS
1982

Printed in the United States of America

For

all my Jesuit confrères at Enghien and Chantilly,
where Teilhard's best was the air we breathed.
But especially for Régis Bernard, Michel Bouillot, André Derville,
and Casimir Gnanadickam, whose spirit still pervades my personal
"Comment je Crois."

Courage, mes vieux! On les aura à la fin. . . .

Abbreviations

AM *The Appearance of Man.* Trans. J. M. Cohen. New York: Harper & Row, 1965 / *L'Apparition de l'homme.* Paris: Editions du Seuil, 1956.

FM *The Future of Man.* Trans. Norman Denny. New York: Harper & Row, 1964 / *L'Avenir de l'homme.* Paris: Editions du Seuil, 1959.

HE *Human Energy.* Trans. J. M. Cohen. New York: Harcourt, Brace, Jovanovich, 1971 / *L'Energie humaine.* Paris: Editions du Seuil, 1962.

HM *The Heart of Matter.* Trans. René Hague. New York: Harcourt, Brace, Jovanovich, 1979 / *Le Coeur de la matière.* Paris: Editions du Seuil, 1976.

PM *The Phenomenon of Man.* Trans. Bernard Wall. New York: Harper & Row, 1959. Rev. ed., 1965 / *Le Phénomène humain.* Paris: Editions du Seuil, 1955.

SC *Science and Christ.* Trans. René Hague. New York: Harper & Row, 1968 / *Science et Christ.* Paris: Editions du Seuil, 1965.

VP *The Vision of the Past.* Trans. J. M. Cohen. New York: Harper & Row, 1966 / *La Vision du passé.* Paris: Editions du Seuil, 1957.

War Writings *Writings in the Time of War.* Trans. René Hague. New York: Harper & Row, 1968 / *Ecrits du temps de la guerre, 1916–1919.* Paris: Grasset, 1965.

Note: All references are given first to the English translation; then, after the slash, to the French original.

Contents

Introduction

WHEN *The Phenomenon of Man* APPEARED in English translation in 1959,[1] it was pelted with a storm of criticism by the Anglo-Saxon scientific community. Two of the best-known reviews of Teilhard's synthetic work, by his friend George Gaylord Simpson, and by the Nobel prizewinner P. B. Medawar,[2] were especially severe, and, in the latter case, surprisingly intemperate. In both cases the attack was aimed at Teilhard's claim to have written a "treatise" which was "purely scientific." So, at least, read the very opening sentence of the English translation, and neither Simpson nor Medawar seems ever to have gotten beyond that very partial description of the work's genre, or checked whether the translator had done justice to the original French.[3] That translation, as it happens, is misleading, and, furthermore, Teilhard goes on from there to define the genre of his work much more precisely than that opening sentence could ever hope to do. The result of ignoring those further qualifications is that the hasty–lazy assumption undergirding Medawar's and Simpson's approach to the work is so thoroughly misguided as to make the majority of their criticisms a series of irrelevancies.[4] Theodosius Dobzhansky, on the other hand, has written kindly about Teilhard's synthesis; perhaps the conti-

[1] This translation, by Bernard Wall, was published in New York by Harper & Row. The French edition dates from 1955. A much needed revision of Wall's original translation was issued in 1965.

[2] Simpson's review appeared in *Scientific American*, 202, No. 4 (April 1960), 201–207. Medawar wrote in *Mind*, 70, No. 277 (January 1961), 99–106.

[3] Medawar writes (p. 100) of one passage in Wall's translation that "here, as almost everywhere else, [it] captures the spirit and sense of the original." The subsequent history of that translation warrants the surmise that Medawar may have brought either competence or care to his comparison with the French, but certainly not both.

[4] Many of those irrelevancies would have been spared us had Medawar and Simpson paid some small attention to Teilhard's methodological observations; see PM 29–36, 53–54, 142–46, 163–64/21–30, 49–50, 154–59, 179–80. See also chap. 9, note 6, below.

nental European tendency to be more sympathetic to the *geist-liche* forms of *Wissenschaft* made him more receptive to the blend of science, poetry, metaphysics, and mysticism he claims to find there. But he gives no specifics to assure us that he really identified the method-spine which gives the work its bone-structure.[5]

The publication of *The Future of Man*, in 1964, prompted the distinguished English philosopher of science, Stephen Toulmin, to re-assess the issue;[6] the central question, Toulmin was astute enough to see, was that of situating the genre in which Teilhard was writing. His tone was quieter, his verdict more moderate; but that verdict, when all is said, was essentially negative: Teilhard was writing a species of "natural theology," of a type more Protestant than Catholic, and even as a professed agnostic Toulmin was compelled to agree with the Dominican Olivier Rabut that the work's merit was seriously questionable at best.

Besides the questions raised by Rabut's own tendentious estimate,[7] and Toulmin's dubious grounds for agreeing with it, there are several oddities in his study which render his conclusions at least suspect. How arbitrary, first of all, to assume that the disparate essays contained in *The Future of Man* would inevitably illumine the genre in which *The Phenomenon of Man* was written; Toulmin can find only two loci in the entire book which bear on the question, surely a slender basis for his sweeping conclusions. This would have been true even if he had gone to the trouble of showing that their genre was uncontestably the same as that of *The Phenomenon of Man*, a step Toulmin never

[5] See his *Mankind Evolving* (New Haven: Yale University Press, 1962), pp. 2, 337, 347–48; his *The Biology of Ultimate Concern* (New York: World, 1969), passim, but esp. pp. 108–37; and his "Pierre Teilhard de Chardin as a Scientist," in Teilhard's *Letters to Two Friends, 1926–1952* (New York: New American Library, 1968), pp. 219–27.

[6] "On Teilhard de Chardin," *Commentary*, 39, No. 3 (March 1965), 50–55.

[7] Toulmin quotes (p. 54) from Rabut's *Teilhard de Chardin: A Critical Study* (New York: Sheed & Ward, 1961), to the effect that "The spiritual perfection of mankind is not the automatic result of Evolution," nor does "evolutionary progress *necessarily* lead to an increase in sanctity" (emphasis Rabut's). Unfortunately for Rabut (and for Toulmin), Teilhard would have agreed with both statements, while questioning the "two-storey" natural–supernatural theology which prompts Rabut's crude misunderstanding of him.

deems it necessary to take. But Toulmin sits uneasily between two stools: he senses that Teilhard may well be claiming to write the kind of "science" humans will be writing in future decades, and yet, to judge whether the man's contentions are "based on science," he takes his norm from the prevalent Neo-Darwinian emphasis in contemporary evolutionary biology, surely loose procedure. Finally, he places Teilhard in the philo-sophic line of Edouard Le Roy and Henri Bergson, but mentions Pierre Duhem only in a deprecatory (and quite misleading) aside;[8] a closer acquaintance with Duhem, along with a more careful reading of the methodological remarks sown plentifully throughout *The Phenomenon of Man*, would have alerted him to the real importance which Duhem's philosophy of science had for the shaping of Teilhard's own "hyperphysical" method.

All of this would have been even more evident had Toulmin awaited the publication of *The Vision of the Past*:[9] no other single volume of Teilhard's works is more revealing on the gene-sis and nature of the method he eventually came to apply in *The Phenomenon of Man*. Chances are that a reading of the essays contained in that work would have changed Toulmin's very way of asking his questions; though what his answers would have been to those more relevant questions, I shall not presume to guess.

But they are important questions, and well worth pursuing— first of all, out of elementary fairness to Teilhard himself. The intellectual world owes such fairness to all its faithful servants, and whether we count him right or wrong, Teilhard must be counted among that number. But more urgently still, this man strove to open a way to bridging the chasm between "scientific" and more humanistic, poetic, and religious modes of envisaging our evolving world, a way in which those seemingly inimical

---

[8] His passing reference (p. 50) to Duhem's essay on the "Physics of a Be-liever" would leave the false impression that the title quoted accurately re-flected Duhem's intentions rather than the highly questionable accusation to which Duhem was replying. See below, chap. 1, note 1.

[9] The French edition of this work had, in fact, predated (1956) the pub-lication of the French edition of FM (1959); but the English editions un-fortunately appeared in the reverse order, in 1966 and 1964, respectively. Writing in 1965, Toulmin takes no account whatever of the French edition of VP, despite Rabut's frequent references to it.

views could converge without becoming confused. Religious fads like "Secular Christian" and "Death of God" theologies may come and go; the labels change, but it seems to go unquestioned that the progress of post-Renaissance science has irreversibly transformed mankind's religious consciousness. Humanity, "come of age," inexorably lives in a "desacralized world," and there is the end of it. So we are told, again and again; little wonder, then, that a man who claimed that "to those who know how to *see*, nothing is profane" would be tacitly shelved as just another quaint anachronism, an old theological hat which no longer fits the human head.

There is no small irony in the picture of a conscientious Dietrich Bonhoeffer in his prison cell, poring over Weizsäcker's portrait of physics and de Kruif's narrative paean to the triumphs of experimentalism, during the very years in which Teilhard, cut off in China by the same war, was busy retouching the manuscript of *The Phenomenon of Man*. Bonhoeffer was making what would seem to be his first protracted attempt at finding out how the scientist went about his business; Teilhard, a practicing scientist for decades, was trying to get both scientists and scientific-minded people to understand why they should radically reform their way of "seeing" things. It is conceivable that both of them were being naïve; it is difficult to see how both of them could simultaneously be right. But if Teilhard be right, the consequences for relating the "two cultures" as well as for reviving our religious sensibilities are enormous.

"Seeing"—*voir*—this is the central term in Teilhard's message to our science-minded century. But he is asking not only the science-minded, but anti-scientifics as well, to learn how to "see." That diversity of "audiences" is one reason why *The Phenomenon of Man* can be a difficult book to read and understand. For Teilhard seldom signposts his remarks as aimed, now at his fellow-scientists, now at that brave but recalcitrant band who feel obliged to resist the pervasive influence of scientific thought-ways; we ourselves are more often obliged to ferret out his addressees, and only then does it become clear what "point" he is making.

That diversity of audiences is more clearly identified in the essays written from 1921 until 1930, which focused on what eventually becomes the "vision of the past" encased in *The Phenomenon of Man*. At times, Teilhard is addressing his fellow-Catholics, in hopes of getting them to "see" the world in the evolutionary terms which alone make sense to his fellow-scientists. Some of these are philosophers battling to preserve a "spiritualistic" view of humanity; some are theologians, loftily proclaiming evolution as "merely a hypothesis." But some of them, like Louis Vialleton, are believing fellow-scientists, corrosively analyzing the evidence for evolution, and concluding that the case is far from proven. But there are other occasions when Teilhard addresses his scientific fellows, as convinced as he is that evolution actually "happened"; to these his message is a different one, and centers largely on "how" evolution must have happened. But, as the following pages will make clear, Teilhard packs more into his message to scientists than that; for they too have things to learn about how, even as reflective scientists, they might come to "see" the evolving world in fresh terms.

The essays we are about to examine help to identify these various audiences as Teilhard turns his attention from one to another and back again. They also permit us to follow, step by step, the process by which Teilhard developed the method he came to label "hyperphysics"—the method he brings to bear in elaborating the "vision" of our evolutionary past which he presents to us in the first three major sections of his synthetic work. The credit we accord to that "vision of the past," Toulmin was alert enough to see, is crucial for appreciating the value of Teilhard's closing recommendations for human survival and progress.

Which brings me to the precise, and precisely limited, aim of this essay. I do not mean to explain or evaluate Teilhard's vision of and prescriptions for the human future, except insofar as it has become necessary to clear him of the accusation that he surreptitiously employed that vision of the future as an unavowed premiss for the validity of his vision of the past.[10] That vision of the past, I hope to show, reposes on evidence and arguments which are logically independent of his very real concern about the future of humanity. But the "evidence" must be examined and "seen" in a certain way, in accord with the canons and

---

[10] See below, pp. 117–32, for treatment of this, Simpson's objection to PM.

exigencies of a method which is, when all is said, remarkably well defined, much more sophisticated than critics have imagined, and carefully justified by a series of considerations rooted in an exploration of the activity of science itself.

But is it really indispensable to ponder these earlier essays in order to uncover the method Teilhard applied in *The Phenomenon of Man*? Strictly speaking, no. After tracing the development of his method in those earlier essays, I shall try to show that a careful reading of *The Phenomenon* itself would have sufficed to enlighten the Medawars, Simpsons, and Toulmins on precisely what Teilhard was, and was not, doing. My aim here is to show how this carefully composed work could, and should, have been read by critics from whom a careful reading might have been expected. But once again, I stress that my analysis here is limited to the way Teilhard earned his right (as he saw it) to present the vision of humanity's evolutionary past along lines which deserve far more serious attention than they have been given.

True, a number of European writers, mostly on the Continent, have consented to study Teilhard more carefully than their peers in the English-speaking world. There have been distinguished essays written on that larger "dialectic," whereby Teilhard endeavored to show the consonance between the Christian vision of the world and the evolutionary view to which his personal hyperphysical exploration brought him.[11] Far fewer writers, however, have concerned themselves precisely with the method subtending that hyperphysical view of evolution;[12] and I know of none who has taken the tack I follow here, of tracing the gradual development of that "hyperphysics" through his earlier essays.[13]

[11] Perhaps the most compelling of these analyses comes from Madeleine Barthélemy-Madaule, in her *La Personne et le drame humain chez Teilhard de Chardin* (Paris: Editions du Seuil, 1967), pp. 13–48.

[12] An important exception is Christian d'Armagnac, especially in his "Philosophie de la nature et méthode chez le Père Teilhard de Chardin," *Archives de Philosophie*, 20, No. 1 (January–March 1957), 4–41. D'Armagnac has also produced a perceptive series of annual roundups on works by and about Teilhard, in the pages of *Etudes*; at points they show that his views have evolved from the position he took in 1957.

[13] No such work, at any rate, has come to my attention, though one or other along these lines may conceivably lie buried amid the pile of university

Not only limited, the task I have assumed is a relatively modest one; I do not lay claim to having brought even it to a full measure of completion. Nor am I deluded into thinking that it will settle henceforth all the disagreements, strident or otherwise, which beset discussions of Teilhard's "hyperphysics." There are too many others much better equipped than I for those subsequent discussions. But it is time that we began, at least, to ask what Teilhard actually said about his method, instead of sending up lazy balloons of fantasy about what he "must" have said and meant. Even this modest beginning may serve to show that close study of this man continues to be worthwhile, and may encourage others, more competent than I can claim to be in such questions, to take that study seriously.

A word in closing on the expository method I have elected to follow. It was at first tempting to let Teilhard "speak for himself," as it were, and merely string together a series of quotations from the English translations of his works, with little more than occasional commentary from me. In fact, a first draft of this essay took very much that form. But, in the end, that mode of exposition proved unworkable. For every quotation had to be extracted from a context which gave it point and conditioned its understanding; the result was an exposition of Teilhard's thought more labored and roundabout than I had imagined it would be. But, secondly, the English translations we have been furnished of Teilhard leave much to be desired: I shall be obliged to point to certain passages which seriously misconstrue the French, but there are a number of other passages, as well, where translators have, doubtless in the interests of "readability," injected a muzziness of expression where Teilhard saw the importance of being quite precise, even technical. Finally, no two translators can be expected to agree in their way of rendering a number of

---

theses to which Father László Polgár calls attention in his indefatigable listings in the *Bibliographia de Historia Societatis Jesu*, which appear annually in the *Archivum Historicum Societatis Jesu*. This annual bibliography would constitute a gold mine for anyone interested in doing a more comprehensive study than I have attempted here. See also Polgár's less complete but admirably selected *Internationale Teilhard-Bibliographie, 1955–1965* (Freiburg & Munich: Alber, 1965), and Joseph M. McCarthy's more recent *Pierre Teilhard de Chardin: A Comprehensive Bibliography* (New York & London: Garland, 1981).

French expressions which recur, and by their recurrence alert us to the fact that the author is using, over and over again, terms which have progressively assumed a technical or semi-technical value which underlines the continuity of his personal thinking.

It became more and more necessary, then, to check the French which lay behind a diversity of translators' renderings. Eventually, the only solution was to work directly with and from the French original—a procedure which should perhaps have been obvious from the beginning, but one which, in any case, I strongly urge upon anyone who wishes to catch the frequently surprising rigor of a thinker who is, alas, too often thought of as having written with more enthusiasm than exactitude.

In the end, I have chosen to proceed largely by paraphrasing rather than by quoting Teilhard; but I hope to have paraphrased him in such a way as to reproduce his thought as faithfully and exactly as could be. In every case, though, I have given precise references to the French originals, with a companion reference to the standard English translation. If comparison between my paraphrase and the English translation sometimes raises questions in the reader's mind, then take that as an unspoken *caveat lector*: please, check the French.

The exploration of Teilhard's earlier essays proceeds chronologically, in the main. But there were times when shifting into a more thematic mode of development either promised greater clarity, or offered other advantages to the reader's understanding; I have tried to indicate such shifts when making them.

For help along the winding path toward completing this study, my debts are so countless as to defy detailed acknowledgment. But I cannot spare mention of: Rev. Vincent T. O'Keefe, s.j., who loyally encouraged and generously supported the pioneer explorations of Fordham University's "Teilhard Research Institute" during the years of his presidency; the late Henry R. Luce and the Ford Foundation, whose financial support was invaluable; Fordham's Philosophy Department and Administration, for granting the several Faculty Fellowships which facilitated research and maturation of this, along with books in other fields; and Mlle Jeanne Mortier, who so courteously and cordially placed the resources of the Fondation Teilhard de Chardin at my disposal. More recently, I have received excellent advice from two of my colleagues specializing in the Philosophy of Science, Drs. Gerrit Smith and Dominic Balestra; for that, warm thanks. Finally, I have been angelically blessed with the services of a typist, Mrs. Karen Harris, and of an editor, Dr. Mary Beatrice Schulte, both of them as seraphically cheerful as they are superbly competent. To these, and to a legion who must remain unnamed, my gratitude, and apologies that this book is less than the far finer product their generous hearts deserve.

Fordham University   ROBERT J. O'CONNELL, S.J.

1
"Seeing":
Teilhard and the "New Positivism"

The Phenomenon of Man has been variously regarded as either an attack on science or an effort to confront the scientist with an apology for Christianity. To anyone entertaining either of these attitudes, it must come as a small surprise, one tinged with an aura of the ironic, to discover that Teilhard's earliest essays on science and evolution betray quite the contrary of those supposed penchants: much of what he ingests into his later method developed precisely out of a determined series of efforts to defend science, and to present his fellow-Catholics with an apologia for the scientific way of "seeing" things.

But Catholics were scarcely the only ones who stood in opposition to evolutionary theory; nor was the anti-scientific animus confined to the proposals advanced by anthropology and paleontology. The suspicion of science, when Teilhard was young, ran both deeper and wider: the burning question toward the beginning of his career was whether science in its entire compass, including even physics, could validly claim to tell us anything about the real world.

The development of science itself, and especially of theoretical physics, was partially responsible for these wholesale doubts. As instruments were developed to make measurements more exact, and investigative methods more refined, confident conclusions which had formerly been drawn from past experiments were cast into doubt; simpler theories were (apparently) discarded, to be replaced by more complex and sophisticated successor-theories; those theories, in turn, became more and more involved in webs of recondite and arcane mathematical formulation. The very language of scientific formulation came progressively to insinuate that it bore only the most tenuous kinship with the "real" world humans dwelt in and dealt with; and the baffling succession of theories and models, newer ones being proposed to replace older, but with the same assertive confidence with which the older had been advanced in the first place, bred the growing suspicion that scientific representations of reality told us more about the workings of the scientific mind than about the reality it purported to work on.

More radically still, it became increasingly plausible, as the celebrated Pierre Duhem had argued, that no experiment, aimed at testing one or other node in the total web of scientific theory, could move one inch without, in practice at least, accepting the vast array of theoretical assumptions which the rest of the scientific web supposed; whereas any of them could be deemed just as questionable in its turn.[1] A century which had once been assured by

[1] Pierre Duhem (1861–1916) was a distinguished physicist as well as an historian and philosopher of science; this "total" view of the testability of any scientific theory was one of his principal contentions, but scarcely the only one of interest to Teilhard, and to us here. In the fifteen months between April 1904 and June 1905, Duhem wrote a series of thirteen articles in the *Revue de Philosophie*, under the general title "La Théorie physique: Son Objet, sa structure." These essays were later collected into a book with the same title, published in Paris by Chevalier & Rivière in 1906. One testimony to the enduring interest of Duhem's proposals is Philip P. Wiener's translation of the second edition of that work (Paris: Rivière, 1914), entitled *The Aim and Structure of Physical Theory*, published by Princeton University Press in 1954 and reissued in paperback by Atheneum in 1962. Wiener's translation includes the two subsequent essays which Duhem placed as appendices to his second edition, on the "Physics of a Believer" and on "The Value of a Physical Theory." Here Duhem was replying to misrepresentations of his earlier contentions (see above, Introduction, note 8, where I find Toulmin making a similarly misleading suggestion).

Teilhard's earliest extant essay on these questions, which we are about to examine, was largely inspired by Duhem's articles in the form which they took in 1904 and 1905. Where important for comparison with Teilhard's early essay, I refer to the text of those original articles in the *Revue de Philosophie*; in all such cases, the translation is my own, but I refer the reader in

Auguste Comte that scientific "positivism" was an infallible program for banishing myths and getting at the "facts" looked back on those halcyon days nostalgic for their lost innocence. A "new" positivism arose to tumble the old from its pedestal; the so-called "facts" of science, its proponents reminded the scientist, were inextricably bound up with a whole network of theoretical patterns; the scientist as such concerned himself not only with getting at the "facts," but with making some patterned sense of them. And dark hints were being uttered that between competing "patterns," one could never really be sure whether any particular scientific pattern had been discovered in or imposed upon, read out of or read into, the behavior of the world. The choice between competing scientific theories might, after all, be an entirely arbitrary affair, far more dependent on the subjectivity of the scientist than on the contours of objective reality.

The earliest essay we have from his pen shows Teilhard already grappling with this problem. The year is 1905; Teilhard is twenty-four years of age, and engaged in that stage of his Jesuit studies devoted to philosophy. But he was also studying physics, one of the subjects he was shortly to teach in the Jesuit *collège* in Cairo; in fact, the indications are that the Society was destining him at the

parentheses to the relevant pages in Wiener's translation of the book's second edition. Where exact comparison is less crucial, I refer merely to Wiener's translation.

To illustrate his contention that it is never a single isolable member of a theory which is subject to evaluation, but the entire ensemble of the theory, Duhem draws a comparison whose interest will become clearer farther on in this study: when someone brings a faulty watch to a watchmaker, Duhem writes, the artisan rightly takes the watch apart and examines each cog and wheel, one after the other. But when a sick man comes to a doctor, the doctor is obliged to "guess at the seat and cause of the sickness only by inspecting the disorders affecting the *entire body*" (emphasis added). The physicist who sets himself to improving on a faulty theory must, Duhem concludes, act much more like a doctor than a watchmaker ("La Théorie physique: Son Objet, sa structure." X. "La Théorie physique et l'expérience," *Revue de Philosophie*, 6, No. 3 (March 1905), 277; *The Aim and Structure of Physical Theory*, trans. Wiener, p. 188).

time for a career as a physicist.[2] It was natural, then, that he approach the problem of scientific knowledge of the real world as it affected physical theory. Hence, the title of his essay: "On the Arbitrary [Element] in the Laws, Theories, and Principles of Physics."[3]

His sketch of the problem as well as his proposed solutions betray a good acquaintance with several contemporary philosophers of science, chief among them the physicist Pierre Duhem.[4] For one thing, Duhem was adamant in restricting the entire realm of scientific knowledge to the "phenomenal" order. The business of science was not that of "explaining" the workings of the real world—the *dessous*, or underlying reality of the observable; that task belonged to philosophy, and more particularly to metaphysics. Science must jealously preserve its own autonomy, and sedulously avoid entanglement in those questions—touching on the "reality" and "nature" of physical entities—about which metaphysicians endlessly argue. Hence, physics must content itself with proposing, not causal, but "phenomenal," laws; with discovering and bringing into order the ways in which the real world "appeared" to act.

That ordering task made it incumbent on the scientist of whatever field to discover wider and more general relationships in the welter of specific phenomenal laws, of limited application, so that their initially bewildering variety could be seen to flow from a relatively small number

---

[2] René d'Ouince, *Un Prophète en procès*, 2 vols. (Paris: Aubier–Montaigne, 1970), I 60n19. The entire chapter on Teilhard's education as a Jesuit is worth reading, particularly to sober those offhand judgments about his "mediocrity" as a philosopher and theologian. The man was clearly better grounded in both these fields than many of his later critics could claim to be.

[3] "De l'Arbitraire dans les lois, théories, et principes de la physique," published in *Quodlibeta* (2 [1905], 247–74), the organ of the Jesuit Scholasticate then at Jersey, and now housed in the library of the Fondation Teilhard, in Paris. I am grateful to Mlle Jeanne Mortier for the opportunity kindly accorded me to profit from the resources contained in that Fondation library.

[4] Teilhard makes a number of explicit references to Duhem's articles in the *Revue de Philosophie*, but his footnotes show he was conversant with the views of Boutroux, Poincaré, Wilbois, and others as well.

of simpler and more general laws. But, Duhem insisted,[5] and Teilhard will echo his insistence to the very end of his career, even these general laws, however fundamental and comprehensive, always stay on the phenomenal level, always bring order into our observations of how things "appear"; science cannot and must not attempt to posture as a philosophy, proposing the underlying "causes" which explain why things act, and indeed must act, the way they do.

Even in the case of historic schools of physical theory whose proponents—like Descartes, Newton, or Huygens—proclaimed that their physical discoveries were "deduced" from their (frequently mechanistic) metaphysic, it is impossible to prove that "the search for [such *metaphysical*] explanation was truly the Ariadne's thread which conducted them in the midst of the confusion of physical laws and enabled them to trace the plan of the labyrinth"—in fact, the history of physics furnished abundant proof to the contrary.[6]

[5] "La Théorie physique: Son Objet, sa structure." I. "Théorie physique et explication métaphysique," *Revue de Philosophie*, 4, No. 4 (April 1904), 389 (*Art and Structure*, trans. Wiener, p. 19; see also pp. 7–8). Duhem's precise point was to keep "physics" as independent of Catholic belief as of any other kind of religious or metaphysical commitment. He is particularly searching in his refutation of the "mechanistic" philosophies of physics so popular at the time, but his opposition to all such metaphysical commitments was based on his belief that physicists (and scientists more generally) should be able to communicate and evaluate each other's theories *as scientists*, without any such extra-scientific considerations' obfuscating the issues between them. This will be Teilhard's consistent hope for "science"; it is ironic, but perhaps understandable, that he wound up being accused of the same "faith bias" as critics claimed to uncover in Duhem, particularly in his anti-mechanism. See the most recent example of incomprehension regarding Teilhard's intentions in Jacques Monod's *Chance and Necessity: An Essay on the Natural Philosophy of Modern Biology*, trans. Austryn Wainhouse (New York: Knopf, 1971), pp. 32–33. Rather than answering the difficulties raised by equating scientific with mechanistic modes of explanation, Monod seems not to have grasped them clearly enough to deal with them. The remainder of this study will show, I hope, that his criticisms of Teilhard are little more than an extended *ignoratio elenchi*.

[6] "La Théorie physique: Son Objet, sa structure." III. "Les Théories représentatives et l'histoire de la physique," *Revue de Philosophie*, 4, No. 6 (June 1904), 644 (*Aim and Structure*, trans. Wiener, p. 32).

It is worth remarking that Duhem's whole case for this autonomy of science is regularly expressed in terms of a stark contrast between physics and metaphysics; the same contrast will mark Teilhard's customary way of expressing himself. Intermediate levels of philosophic discourse, like cosmology, are either ignored or implicitly considered as "deductions" from metaphysics. Even more to the point, neither Teilhard nor Duhem ever expressly situates "science" with respect to the level of discourse on which they both regularly move, a level which is clearly that of the more recent discipline, the "philosophy of science." This simplified way of putting the question—is it science or metaphysics, as though no gray area existed between them —will occasion a number of misunderstandings for Teilhard in later years; but many of those misunderstandings arise from his flattering assumption that his fellow-scientists were as alert and reflective as he had come to be on the epistemological problems embedded in the practice of their art.

Even when confined to this phenomenal level, however, a "reality problem" exists for science generally, and even for what then appeared the very queen of the sciences, mathematical physics. Consider, for example, the physical laws of falling bodies, and the way they are arrived at. Still largely indebted to Duhem, Teilhard reminds his readers that any particular experiment aimed at uncovering the quantitative relationships accompanying any and every instance of fall inevitably produces measurements which only approximate the "ideal" law the mathematical physicist eventually comes up with. But the physicist performs a number of these experiments, each of them producing similarly approximate results, and then "fairs off" the results mathematically; he proposes a single mathematical formula to express *the* law of falling bodies in exact terms, and attributes the difference between his approximate measurements and this exact result to "experimental error." But this entire process betrays the fact that the physicist has gone about his task with an (often unrecognized) mixture of experimental observation and mathematical faith, the latter constantly "correcting" the imprecision and approximations which continually beset the results of his experimental observations. How does the physicist actually *choose* among the variety of approximate results his experiments yield? He does so, Teilhard replies, out of a conviction that nature behaves in a manner which can be formulated, mathematically, in "simple" terms; and the simpler those formulas are, the more the physicist is confident they express the behavior of natural realities. Or, to put the same proposition in visual terms: the physicist is confident that "ideal" experimental results will always "graph" perfectly; in consequence, any experimental measurement which falls above his ideal graph-line he counterbalances with another experimental result falling below that line. Indeed, any reading which diverges crazily from his ideal graph-line he feels entitled simply to discount, as so absolutely "out of line" that it *must* be due to equipment failure or human error.

On what basis, then, does the physicist make his "choice"? Most routine physicists will reply, unreflectively, that their choice of the "law" they formulate is based on the "facts," but this is patently not the case. For the concrete "facts" are more closely represented by the whole series of individual pointer-readings which result, each from an individual experiment, and each representing only an "approximation"—if that—to the "ideal" pointer-reading called for by the "law" and its "ideal graph-line." If the "concrete facts" were master, the physicist would never succeed in formulating an "exact" law. His whole procedure brings the physicist to transform these concrete, approximate "facts" into idealized, schematized, "abstract" facts, the only kind which can "verify" the sort of exact law he is bent on uncovering.

But, one might conclude, if the physicist's "choice" of the exact mathematical formula to express the "law" of any and all falling bodies is not based on the "facts," it must be an "arbitrary" choice; now, at least, the point of Teilhard's essay title is clear. But does it mean that he draws this precise conclusion? Not quite, as we shall see.

Even when verifying experimental laws, accordingly, the physicist is always making educated "choices" about what he will count as "evidence." But "choice" plays even a larger role when it comes to accepting one of several competing "theories" of physics. Is this choice always, or ever, commanded by "logical" grounds?

Writing in italics, Duhem answers in the negative. For why could the physicist not symbolize "either several distinct groups of experimental laws, or even a single group of laws, by means of *several theories*, each one of which depends on hypotheses *irreconcilable* with those on which the others depend?"—and he answers, again in italics, and capitals,

> IF THE QUESTION IS TO BE ANSWERED BY INVOKING ONLY REASONS OF PURE LOGIC, the physicist cannot be prevented from representing, either different ensembles of laws, or even a single group of laws, by several irreconcilable theories;

if pure "logic" be at the helm, then "incoherence in physical theory *cannot* be condemned."[7]

And yet physicists would, almost universally, be uncomfortable with such theoretical incoherence; they all experience the need for logical coordination in physical theory. That felt need, Duhem goes on to show, is required neither by the principle of contradiction nor by the law of economy of thought. And yet, physical theorists feel, and rightly, that it is somehow justified. How? "It is legitimate" to re-

---

[7] "La Théorie physique: Son Objet, sa structure." V. "Les Théories abstraites et les modèles mécaniques (2)," ibid., 5, No. 2 (September 1904), 258 (*Aim and Structure*, trans. Wiener, pp. 100–101).

quire such logical coordination because the opinion demanding it "results from an innate sentiment in us, which it is impossible to justify by purely logical considerations, yet which it is impossible to snuff out entirely"; "every physicist aspires naturally toward the unity of science," toward a "logical unity in physical theory."[8]

But what warrant is there for trusting this "aspiration" toward coherence and unity in science? Though more tentative in flavor, Teilhard's proposed conclusion faithfully reflects a second of Duhem's impressive insights. The answer comes in stages: first, the physicist's entire procedure is commanded by an "instinct for simplicity." No "logic" can be brought forward to validate that instinct, but it operates, in part, on identifiably "aesthetic" grounds.

> Wherever order rules, it brings beauty along with it. Theory, therefore, not only makes the ensemble of physical laws it represents easier to handle, more convenient, more useful; it makes it more beautiful, too.

> It is impossible to follow the steps [*marche*] of one of Physics' great theories, watching it start from initial hypotheses and then in regular deductions majestically unfold a series of consequences which represent, down to the minutest detail, a host of experimental laws, without being taken by the beauty of such a construction, without vividly experiencing [the truth] that such a creation of the human spirit is truly a work of art.[9]

But, Duhem goes on to argue, "that aesthetic emotion is not the only sentiment inspired by a theory brought to a high degree of perfection. [A theory in this state] persuades us of more: persuades us to view it as a *natural classification*."[10]

[8] Ibid., 261–62 (*Aim and Structure*, trans. Wiener, pp. 103–104).

[9] "La Théorie physique: Son Objet, sa structure." II. "Théorie physique et classification naturelle," *Revue de Philosophie*, 4, No. 5 (May 1904), 549 (*Aim and Structure*, trans. Wiener, p. 24).

[10] Ibid.

The term becomes central to Teilhard's subsequent thinking and writing. It is suggestive, in this regard, that Duhem finds it helpful to illustrate how he means it by adducing an example, not from physics, but from the life sciences. The "naturalist," he tells us, considers the various "species" of living beings, and

> orders them in groups, more particular groups subordinated to more general; to form these groupings, he considers the various organs, the vertebral column, the cranium, heart, digestive tract, lung, natatory air-bladder. He considers them, not in the particular and concrete form they take in each individual, but in the abstract, general, schematic form appropriate to all the species of the same group. He sets up comparisons between these organs, transfigured by abstraction; he notes analogies and differences . . . purely ideal kinships which bear, not on real organs, but on generalized and simplified conceptions formed in the naturalist's own mind; the [resulting] classification is nothing but a synoptic table furnishing a résumé of all these kinships.

> When the zoologist affirms that such a classification is natural, he means that these ideal linkages, established by reason between abstract conceptions, correspond to real relations between the concrete beings in which these abstractions are embodied; he means, for example, that the more or less striking resemblances he has noted between different species are indicators of a kinship between the individuals composing those species, a kinship which, more or less close, he understands in the proper sense of that term. [He means to affirm] that the bracketings whereby he represents for the [reader's] eye the subordination of classes, orders, families, genera, reproduce the branchings of the genealogical tree whereby the different vertebrates came forth from the same stalk. . . . [W]hen he contemplates the order which his comparative procedures have introduced into the confused crowd of animals, the anatomist is incapable of not affirming these relationships; [but] the proof of that affirmation transcends his methods. And even were the physiologist and paleontologist to demonstrate to him one day that the kinship he has imagined cannot be, that the transformist hypothesis is a con-

struct of his imagination, he would continue to believe that
the plan sketched by his classification represents real relationships between the animals in question; he would admit to
having been mistaken on the nature, but not on the existence,
of those relationships.[11]

So too in physics, Duhem suggests; despite the sometimes airy abstractions with which it works, despite the
idealizing character of mathematics and geometry,

> the ease with which each experimental law finds its place in
> the classification the physicist has erected, the dazzling clarity
> which spreads over an ensemble so perfectly ordered, per-
> suade us invincibly that such a classification is not purely
> artificial, that an order of this sort did not result from some
> purely arbitrary grouping, imposed on the laws in question
> by some ingenious organizer.

> Without being able to give an account of our conviction,
> and still, without being able to give it up, we see in the exact
> arrangement of such a system the mark whereby a *natural
> classification* is recognized. . . . we sense that the groupings
> our theory has established correspond to real affinities be-
> tween the realities themselves.[12]

The aspiration toward unity and coherence in scientific
theory, Duhem concludes, is the "inseparable companion

[11] Ibid., 550 (*Aim and Structure*, trans. Wiener, p. 25). Wiener mistrans-
lates a key phrase here. Duhem writes that the scientist, once he surveys the
order which his classificatory efforts have "introduced" into the previously
chaotic welter of specimens, *ne peut ne pas affirmer ces rapports*, "cannot *not*
affirm those relationships" (scil., as reflecting real relationships among the
specimens themselves)—and that, *despite* the fact that the "proof" of any such
affirmation "transcends his methods" (scil., as a *scientist*). Wiener's "he cannot assert these relations, the proof of which transcends his methods" omits
the vital double negative, thereby burying the important paradox of scientific
activity Duhem is stressing. It could just be that Wiener found it difficult to
credit that Duhem was making this paradoxical claim, but clearly he is, and
it is vital to his argument. The attribution of "reality value" to any scientific
classification is an affirmation which transcends science itself; hence, the need
for a reflective "philosophy of science."

[12] Ibid., 550–51 (*Aim and Structure*, trans. Wiener, pp. 25–26). Wiener
oddly omits the italics, *classification naturelle*, which Duhem thought it important to use in his French version.

real itself have "every chance" of being one and the same (*War Writings* 162/184).

Whatever one may think of his reasoning as presented here—and Teilhard makes no pretense of spelling out adequately his grounds for having eventually opted for this scientific realism—it must be supposed a serious and honest option: the lifelong sacrifice which came with it is now a matter of historical record. It would have been far more comfortable to stay—as many Catholics did—with the dualistic breach between mind and reality which he had long entertained. It would have absolved him from the duty which he subsequently felt was his, that of striving in season and out to get the theologians of his day to admit to what his option entailed: that Evolution was, not merely a "hypothesis" in the feeblest sense of that term, not merely a scientific "representation" of a reality which could well be otherwise, but the way things actually were. It was, in short, his very "belief in science" which brought down on him the various measures of suspicion, exile, censorship, and silence which Church authorities meted out to him for the last thirty years of his life—a large price to pay for honesty, but grounds for suspecting that the man was at least as honest as some who have thought fit to write him off as self-deceived and bent on deceiving others.

But this early essay suggests other considerations as well. It was significant that Duhem chose to select his illustration for the idea of a "natural classification" from the life sciences, which were to occupy Teilhard in later years. The evidence of the essays written during those years weighs heavily toward indicating that this was the path which Teilhard's mind followed in coming to the "realistic" theory of scientific knowledge which his eventual "belief" in science implied. The criteria of coherence and homogeneity have the aesthetic ring Duhem so unashamedly proposed as the marks, not only of beauty, but of scientific truth as well. But it should be remarked that Duhem's argument tends to be far more compelling to one who has labored through the process of discovery, has gone through the steps of surveying what first appears a chaotic welter of heterogeneous details lacking all relationship with each other, tried one, then another, an entire series of "keys" to uncover the order underlying that chaos, until a key is hit upon, and gradually honed to the shape designed to unlock that underlying order. Duhem's "argument" (if argument it really is) assumes its fullest cogency only to someone who has gone through some such process of initial bafflement, successive approximations, and culminating *eureka*. To the scientist who has had some such discovery experience Duhem describes that *experience* in such reminiscent terms as to provoke the shock of recognition; to one who has never experienced the thrill of discovery, however, even to the routine scientist who has for years worked conscientiously "by the book" of what he takes to be "scientific method," Duhem's description is likely to fall on deaf ears.

But something quite analogous occurs when a scientist finds one, then another, then other anomalies cropping up to disturb the symmetries of a classification which, until that moment, had passed muster as a "natural" one. At that point, the search for another "more natural" classification is on, and the scientist bothered by the anomalies embedded in the older classification may not even have the terms available to share his botheration with those of his fellows who remain tranquilly contented with that older classification. Like the experience of discovery, the experience of botheration is communicable, but often in more limited ways than the creative, as against the routine, scientist would like.

How could the more "routine" scientist be brought to some greater sensitivity to what goes on in these revolutionary moments of scientific "paradigm shift"? An acquaintance with the history of science would be of some help, and Duhem subsequently took that route with his multi-volume work on "World Systems."[16] While not another route entirely, this early probe of Teilhard's will have something of the same effect on his scientific thinking. For once he had confronted and pondered the element of the "arbitrary" in mathematical physics, Teilhard was forever liberated from the nearly bewitching intimidation which that most "scientific" of the sciences seems to exert on the less tutored mind. That air of rigorous exactitude was, after all, to some extent a construct, and within certain limits, at least, illusory. Similarly, the cloak of inexorability, necessity, and iron determinism worn by physical laws and theories was no more than that: it was woven far more by the mathematical "form" of thought contributed by our human minds when they insisted that the zigzag graphs of approximate results "fair off" into ideal sine curves, parabolas, or perfectly straight lines.[17] Could there, beneath this cloak of apparent determinism, exist instead a bubbling sea of spontaneity and indeterminism? Teilhard will later formulate exactly that suggestion; but the grounds for it have already been laid in this early essay.

Can reality, then, be quite the reverse of science's depiction of it? Teilhard never goes to so wild an extreme, and his refusal to do so testifies to the sanity of the man's judgment. The myth of science as a gigantic discovery machine devised for "getting at the facts" was too naïve to bear close investigation; the facts science deals with are already schematized and idealized versions of the concrete reality from which observation takes its initial cues. And yet, Teilhard suggests (though the analogy is my own), the dialogue the scientist carries on with concrete reality is a

[16] Duhem never brought his multi-volume *Systèmes du monde* to completion, but his erudition on the history of scientific theories was awesome. For an analogous historical approach to these questions, see Thomas S. Kuhn's more recent *The Structure of Scientific Revolutions* (Chicago: The University of Chicago Press, 1962; 2nd rev. ed., 1970), and the spate of discussion prompted by that work. See also the Afterword, note 20, below.

[17] Again, the ideas are vintage Duhem; see *Aim and Structure*, trans. Wiener, pp. 134–35.

two-way dialogue: though much of the language is elaborated and contributed by the scientific mind, the scientist is nonetheless listening to what reality says in answer to his scientific questions. He may not always be aware of his insistence that reality talk back in a language which is to some extent at least a foreign tongue; reality's "answers" in that foreign tongue we may not be entitled to take "literally." But if the dialogue succeeds in eliciting an answer, or, better, a series of answers from reality, we may be in a position to decipher, to "translate," those answers, and thereby descry what reality might be uttering in its own native language.

Apply this analogy of "dialogue" to the procession of diverse scientific "models," later replacing earlier ones, which seem to clutter the museum we call the history of science. Take any earlier model "literally," and its replacement by a later might seem to argue that the earlier one was simply "wrong"—leaving us with the uneasy feeling that its later replacement might someday be discarded as equally "wrong" as well; and the conclusion is, science at no point in its advance tells us anything reliable about the way reality truly works. That view of science's historic advance, Teilhard suggests as early as this essay, is sorely questionable:[18] the mistake involved occurs in that initial step of taking *any* scientific model "literally." Indeed the very procession of models which would appear at first to argue for a skeptical attitude toward all scientific knowledge may actually cut a path to the opposite conclusion.

For if, instead of taking any single model "literally,"

[18] Duhem uses an illustration here which may well have imbedded itself in Teilhard's imagination: "by a continuous tradition, each physical theory passes to its successor the share of natural classification it was able to construct, just as, in certain games of antiquity, each runner handed the lighted torch to the runner coming after him; that continuous tradition assures science of unending life and progress" ("Les Théories représentatives et l'histoire de la physique," 645 [*Aim and Structure*, trans. Wiener, pp. 32–33]). Teilhard will apply this relay metaphor to the process of evolution itself: the evolution of science apes the evolution of reality.

we place it in line with its predecessors and successors, then step back to survey the entire series, we may "see" something which escaped our eye before. There may suddenly appear a congeries of factors common to all these models; the presence of those common factors may safely argue to the presence, *in* the reality being investigated, of properties at least analogous to them, factors which reality itself "imposes" on any and every scientific model which is destined to pass the test of experimental verification. The first experimental test may seem rudimentary when compared to its more sophisticated and demanding successors; but the persistence of certain common factors throughout the entire historical series of "successful" models may be the clue to what reality itself is saying in the variety of languages in which this variety of models addresses it.

This cluster of "reality features" insinuated by the factors common to the entire parade of more and more successful models Teilhard refers to here as the "objective residue"; he will later speak of the "imposed factors" which reality must possess, and reveal to scientific probes, if the historic series of more and more successful models is to become intelligible. He suggests an illustration: we may not be obliged to trust in the exactitude claimed for this or that ideal sine-curve law concerning light, but the history of optical research may ground our confidence in saying there must be "something sinusoidal" not only about all light formulas, but about the behavior of light itself.[19]

Again there is a small irony embedded in Teilhard's conclusions: science, he comes down to warning us, is not to be taken "literally" in what it seems to be telling us about the real world; any and all scientific accounts of reality present us with matter for discernment, deciphering, translation. Deprecation of science, one might be tempted to expostulate; but no, Teilhard replies, the only intelligent way to "save science," once all the assumptions

19 Compare Duhem in *Aim and Structure*, trans. Wiener, pp. 26–27.

and implications of scientific procedure are taken into account.

It might be objected that I have drawn a great deal out of a mere schoolboy essay. But when the schoolboy is already twenty-four years of age, and as gifted as Pierre Teilhard de Chardin, that objection loses a great deal of its force. Moreover, the earliest speculations one goes through on a question of serious philosophic import have a way of scribing enduring pathways on one's subsequent thinking: and the choice of Pierre Duhem's remarkably durable views on scientific theory was, at the very least, a singularly fortunate one for Teilhard. But these observations serve only to create a presumption: if this essay be as significant as I suggest it is for understanding the development of Teilhard's later method, those later writings must be allowed to disprove or substantiate that view.

2

Seeing
With an Educated Eye

TEILHARD'S EARLY CONTACT with Duhem's philosophy of science left him purged of any naïve notions about the relationship between "concrete facts" and scientific theory. Even had any residues endured of that view of scientific procedure, they would scarcely have survived the withering fire of anti-evolutionist polemic which, on his return from the First World War, he felt called upon to answer.

By this time his scientific orientation has changed: the Society of Jesus which had originally destined him for physics has now encouraged him to undertake studies in paleontology and geology. Those studies have confirmed his dawning conviction that the scientific picture of our universe as an evolving universe was sound and true, and that theologians and believers who continued to question that view were doing, however good their intentions, a profound disservice to the Church's mission to their scientific-minded contemporaries. In 1923, however, his fellow–Catholic Louis Vialleton, professor of anatomy at Montpellier, had mounted a broadside attack on the proofs then being offered for transformist theory.[1]

Teilhard does not treat all three targets of Vialleton's attack—embryology, comparative anatomy, and systematics—equally; he moves primarily to the defense of the way in which comparative anatomy and more especially systematics come to "see" the temporal series of later liv-

[1] See his *Membres et ceintures des vertébrés tétrapodes: Critique morphologique du transformisme* (Paris: Doin, 1924). A good summary and partial critique can be found in M. Manquat's "Une Critique du transformisme," *Revue des Questions Scientifiques*, 85, No. 2 (April 1924), 370–87.

ing forms as emerging, more highly developed, from their predecessors. The "illusion" of transformism is created, Vialleton argued, by focusing on this or that "evolving" *part*—a limb or wing—rather than on the whole animal, which must have been involved in whatever development may have taken place; that illusion is confirmed by arranging the various "successive" forms in such a way as to suggest that they evolved gradually and continuously (as the mechanistic cast of the theory required), and in relatively "straight lines," through a series of intermediary forms. But the lines are never quite "straight," later species representing as many divergences from as continuations of their alleged predecessors. There are always yawning gaps in the series; intermediary forms must always be imagined to fill those gaps, for the evidence that such intermediary forms ever existed is never produced. And, finally, the fossil record confronts us, generally speaking, only with evidence of fixed, stable forms.

Though questioning the way certain of the "facts" of fossil evidence had been misrepresented, Vialleton's argument focused on the evolutionary "pattern" adduced by the prehistorian to make sense of those facts. Even before Vialleton's book provoked his essay on "The Transformist Paradox," Teilhard was sensitive to this point.[2] He speaks at times as though science did nothing more than unroll the "film" of cosmic events as they occurred, but those expressions are always meant to counter the opinion that science claims to dethrone philosophy as the ultimate "explanation" of things; its competence, he tirelessly repeats, is limited to establishing the sequence of phenomenal antecedents and consequents. But the process of establishing the sequence, he saw from the beginning, was far more like picking up snippets of someone else's film from the cutting-room floor, examining them, and then imaginatively divin-

---

[2] His essay (from the year 1921) on "How the Transformist Question Presents Itself Today" makes this clear; see VP 7–25/15–40.

ing how they could be put together to result in the meaning-
ful work of cinematic art one presumed they must originally have constituted. One has to take into account the
morphological peculiarities, the chronological situation,
and the geographical location of each fossil find in question—something which already supposed acceptance and
creative application of a vast interconnected skein of biological, geological, and geographical theories. Then, once
all these have been taken into account, a host of such finds
has to be arranged into groups and series which would
make intelligible why each form was found at just such a
geological stratum at just this geographical point.

Once their morphological, temporal, and geographical
distribution is taken into account, the solution becomes
clear: various forms of living beings have succeeded, replaced, "relayed" each other in the sequence of bygone
ages; their growth accretions can be made the "*object of a
history*" (VP 22/36; emphasis Teilhard's).[3] What the prehistorian first beheld as a confused crowd has yielded up
the secret of its arrangement: an order which is the result
of periodic laws working by rules which are "exact, simple, and invariable" after all. The process which resulted
in that ordered arrangement must have been (in an echo
of Duhem's criterion) a "natural" one for this initially bewildering profusion of life forms to have settled into such
a detectable arrangement; the whole effect betrays unmistakably that it resulted from a process of "growth."
To make sense of this array of fossil evidence, the prehistorian is right to postulate some "physical connection"
between the successive items before his gaze, a connection
which implies that later forms suppose and replace earlier
in such a way that "none could have appeared earlier or
later" than it actually did (VP 14–15, 20–22/26–27, 33–
36).

---

[3] Cohen's "substance of a history" is a trifle strong; Teilhard is referring to
"history" here as a mode of investigative study.

But, Teilhard admits (he is writing for the general read-ership of *Etudes*), it takes an educated eye to uncover the pattern in the "facts" to which the "untrained eye" remains blind; the "gaze" must be "informed" before it will see that evolution was the "only possible explanation" of the evi-dence (VP 13–14, 20/25, 33; see also, on the same theme, VP 183/257 and AM 49–50/71–73).[4]

Teilhard's problem with the readers of *Etudes* is much the same as his earlier one: explaining how the stages lead-ing up to a "natural classification" leaves the discoverer with so unshakeable a sense of having discerned the lines of reality itself. It takes a complex, sophisticated argument to spell out for the uninitiate how much, and how com-pellingly, the prehistorian "sees" in one protracted gaze of his educated "eye." We are far from the innocent fancy that "evolution is a fact" which anyone can "see." But Vialleton's attack will force Teilhard to reflect even more closely on the process whereby he and his fellow-scientists became convinced (often without examining their grounds as closely as he is now compelled to do[5]) that the "facts" imposed the evolutionary hypothesis as the only pattern for making sense of them.

For Vialleton had succeeded in pointing to the evolu-tionary lines which appeared both rigid and fixed; whereas earlier transformist theories would lead one to expect to uncover suppleness and mobility of evolutionary flow, he had persuasively underlined the fact that evolution's an-ticipated fluidity and continuity broke up, under closer examination, into groupings which seemed, rather, stable, discontinuous, and independent of each other (VP 82/ 118). There were yawning gaps between species which

---

[4] The importance of this appropriate disposition of the "eye" in order to see properly has been ably highlighted in Thomas King's *Teilhard's Mysticism of Knowing* (New York: Seabury, 1981), pp. 44–45, 151n3. On some reserva-tions I have concerning King's overall interpretation, see my review in *Theo-logical Studies*, 43, No. 1 (March 1982), 160–62.

[5] See his remark to this effect in VP 7/18.

were originally envisaged as running continuously into one another; and, Vialleton had argued, it was flying in the face of probability to suppose that some organic bridge could be established between them. No serious morphologist, for instance, would attempt to draw lines of unbroken derivation from reptile to bird, or from walking carnivore to seal (VP 82/118).

Teilhard has profited from his earlier study of difficulties which provoked analogous doubts in mathematical physics: an earlier theoretical model has shown its inadequacy on closer observation, just as the mathematical physicist's application of more refined calculations and measurements uncovered the approximate character of earlier, simpler, physical "laws," and bred at least a temporary doubt about the truth of those earlier laws (VP 90/127). So here, closer and more refined observations have brought naturalists to detect "anomalies" which their older, and simpler, reconstructions of the past would not lead us to expect (VP 81/116–17). But this procession of models should present no greater a difficulty than the procession of models in mathematical physics. For we should fully expect the older model to be a "first approximation"—a simpler "curve" of graphing the process of evolutionary development; it should occasion little surprise and less consternation when more detailed and refined study calls for a more complex and refined model. And yet, one should be alert enough to see that the curve of the earlier model did, after all, resemble to some extent the curve actually followed by nature; older and newer models, he is implying, both share characteristics in common. Draw a map, his first essay had suggested, to the scale of one to a thousand, and the "clusters" on such a map will show up as more scattered on a map scaled one to a hundred. His argument here is substantially the same. Lines of continuous development on the earlier map show up, on closer inspection, to be discrete fibers more divergent from each other than originally imagined—

just as one might have expected. But the message of both models, once properly translated, is substantially the same: they both express the "movement" of life's development.

So much for the replacement of an earlier, simpler, model by a later, more refined and complex, model; what of Vialleton's claim that the fossil evidence showed no proof of actual development? Teilhard changes his analogy. Take a closeup snapshot of any segment of a movement, and the effect is precisely as Zeno argued thousands of years ago. You get a "still," like the picture printed on a single frame of movie film; the fluid, unbroken movement has been broken up into separate segments, each of them rigid and immobile in appearance. But the rigidly immobile is illusion; the fluid movement remains the fact (VP 82–83/117–18).

What, though, of the "gaps" in the fossil record? Here again, Teilhard argues, we are faced with what we should have expected: for the "peduncle"—the array of early transitional forms—always undergoes a kind of automatic "destruction" which leaves no traces of it in the fossil record. That automatic disappearance from the fossil record is explained by the fact that such transitional forms are always small, small both in number and in individual size. It should be no surprise, accordingly, given the vast gaps in the fossil record more generally—gaps even greater than Vialleton pointed out—that such a fragile and diminutive "link" should disappear from the view of a researcher working at a distance from it measured in thousands upon thousands of years (VP 93/130–31).

Despite these gaps, then; despite the appearance of rigid immobility in any close-up segment; despite the complication of earlier, simpler, models of the evolutionary process, the prehistorian, like Teilhard, remains convinced that the fossil record points to the reality of evolution. Why? Again, the echoes of Duhem ring clear: the life-forms in the temporal series, when viewed at sufficient distance (and by the prehistorian's educated eye), are "seen" as succeeding each other in a "rigorously determined order," no form ever reaching full maturity without some preceding form acting as a preliminary "sketch" for it; instead of a chaotic welter, the informed eye detects just that "ordered, organized, and ineluctable distribution of living beings through time and space" which the mind spontaneously takes as representing a "natural distribution." More complicated now than formerly, the scientific reconstruction of this evolutionary process remains, for the paleontologist, no less compelling than in its earlier, simpler, form. And the reason for that conviction remains, for Teilhard, as Duhem had once explained it (VP 84–89/119–26).[6]

The essence of the transformist hypothesis, Teilhard concludes, must not be confused with one or other theory—Darwinian or Lamarckian—adduced to explain its mechanism; *that* evolution took place is beyond serious dispute, but *how* it took place is still matter for continued discussion. But uncertainties about the "how" do not undermine the certainty of the "that." And yet, he is compelled in the end to avow, there may be more to Vialleton's objections than that: identify evolutionary theory with its mechanistic explanation of *how* evolution works (as Vialleton seems to have identified them) and there may be something inexplicable about evolution after all. This sets Teilhard off, as early as the year 1924, on a series of considerations which come to fruition only some years later. It will be best, at the moment, to postpone them until a later chapter in our study of his method and its development.

[6] The change of expression, natural "distribution" for natural "classification," is consistent with the evolutionary view already insinuated by Duhem's own illustration drawn from "natural history" and with his insistence that the logical relationships commending a scientific classification as "natural" must reflect "ontological" relationships among the specimens so classified. See above, chap. 1.

3

Seeing "Wholes"

ONE PARTICULAR TACTIC Vialleton employed in his anti-evolutionary polemic was to invite his readers to focus, at close range, on this or that segment of the fossil record. Seen at close range, each segment took on an air of relative rigidity and fixity; at the same time the gaps between any two such segments seemed to argue for their relative independence of and discontinuity from each other. Teilhard's counterthrust consisted in asking those same readers to take the sort of view which, he is implicitly convinced, the evolutionist prehistorian, in fact, habitually takes, even if he is not always reflectively conscious of doing so. The concluding sections of his reply to Vialleton bring this requirement of scientific "seeing" to more explicit articulation.

The more ordinary way of understanding the activities of science, he admits, would tend more to stress the analytic and regressive character of their procedures. Science, generally, endeavors to explain the actions of larger wholes in terms of their more elementary, molecular, then atomic, then subatomic parts; so too, the tendency to explain the actions of collective entities as the sum of the actions of the individuals composing them (VP 98/137). The advantages of this mode of procedure are undeniable, Teilhard admits, but one may wonder whether it does not stand in need of a complementary way of viewing reality. To make the scientific picture of evolution intelligibly comprehensible, we may have to complement that atomistic method by taking into consideration those properties of collectivities *as such*, properties "which neither the analysis nor the sum of elementary forces could ever account for." We may be compelled to stand back from our examination of the elemental parts to take a view of all terrestrial life "considered as forming a specific whole" and rooted in its activity in the terrestrial world, itself considered as a "whole" (VP 98–100/137–40).

Teilhard's proposal in this instance has a somewhat surprising ring: for instead of reminding his fellow-evolutionists that they do, in fact, take something very like this long-range view of "wholes"—and that the compelling nature of that view is what sustains their theory against such objections as Vialleton's—he makes it sound as though he were proposing something quite novel in the way of "doing science." That implication might be considered all the more surprising in that the Teilhardian penchant for seeing the "whole" dates from his earliest extant writings, the essays written during the First World War. But there, it took a markedly mystical tinge, and Teilhard may be betraying his consciousness of that. But an essay published in *Etudes*[1] in 1921 on (of all things) geology shows that same inclination already working in high gear, and on scientific materials. He means to get his readers quite literally to gaze upon "The Face of the Earth," as the Austrian geologist Suess had termed it. The words of his title, Teilhard assures his readers, express, not some romantic fallacy, but the actual "results reached by geological science" during the past fifty years. It may, and must, be said that the earth has a "physiognomy, a countenance, a face" (VP 26/41) whose features we are "just beginning to decipher." The geological syntheses of Suess and others invite us to see our earth not as just an assemblage of disparate details unrelated to each other—an eye here, a nose there—but as organically related "features" which assume "meaning for our eyes" precisely when we adjust our vision to behold them as such. Again, his intent is to inform, to

[1] "The Face of the Earth," reprinted in VP (26–46/41–70).

"educate" his readers' non-scientific eyes to regard the earth as a geologist like Suess would.

He proceeds to show that to understand the formation of mountains one may have to take into account the contractions of our earthly globe *as a whole*, consider the several great "Alpine" mountain ranges as a single "system," and entertain the possibility that there may be some general law of "crystallization" which works for planets precisely as such. Only in that way can we succeed in making the form which our planet has taken clear and intelligible to both eyes and "minds" (VP 30, 33, 43/48, 51, 64).

This, he claims, is not futuristic projection; the concerted efforts of geological scientists have already succeeded in fitting together the formerly "disjointed features" of the earth's topography until they take on a unitary aspect. Those features, one is tempted to say, have composed themselves, as it were, into a settled facial expression, to which each distinct feature may contribute; but the expression itself must be "read" as the expression of the whole "face." This way of beholding the earth implies that our beholding minds attain to this result only at the price of "lending" to the earth some of our own human sense of "unity," by consenting to allow our intelligence to "infuse" a kind of life into this "material mass." The specters of subjectivism and anthropomorphism have been deliberately raised and candidly acknowledged. What makes the resulting picture so convincing, though, is the allure of "natural classification" which shines out from it; the "network of relationships" geologists have uncovered by viewing the earth this way reveals itself as both "solid" and "true." The ultimate justification of this quasi-anthropomorphic technique of "seeing" may not yet be in Teilhard's grasp, but he will later spell it out more boldly: only when the human observer consciously exploits the evolutionary "kinship" we enjoy, not only with the biological realm, but with the earth itself which gave us birth, can the earth be "seen" as it truly is.[2]

But for such knowledge to emerge, the eye must be accustomed to seeing things as "wholes." It is significant, again, that a principle of his later hyperphysical method, one which could so easily deteriorate into the pathetic fallacies of romanticism, was brought to the surface of Teilhard's more scientific writings precisely because he needed it to defend the evolutionary constructions of science itself. Unlike so many other evolutionists of his day, Teilhard could not afford to brush off the skeptics with a lordly *odi profanum vulgus*; he strained every nerve to meet their skepticism, to illumine them, to train their eye to *see* as the informed scientist had come to see. And Vialleton in particular compelled him to bring to his defense of science a refinement of analysis of which few of his fellow-scientists would have been capable.

The scientist does, Teilhard is convinced, see each life form in its connections with the whole; he simply has not reflected on, and drawn out all the implications of, that methodological fact. Of it, Teilhard might well have said what he said of the connected "postulate" underlying "all modern scientific research": namely, that to be drawn into the web of scientific thinking, "everything must extend its empirical roots indefinitely backward and in all directions."

---

[2] He begins to orchestrate this insight in the essays on "Hominization" and "The Phenomenon of Man" which we shall examine shortly. Note that although Teilhard does not explicitly use the term "natural classification," his mind is clearly working with this scientific aspiration in view. See, for example, his question about purely "accidental features" which might conceivably be "individual" to our earth and, hence, never become truly "intelligible to our minds" (VP 43/64); his hope of attaining to that "ideal of every science," the "deduction of the earth's physiognomy," starting from a few simple givens" (VP 44/65); and, finally, the hope that the scientific mind may eventually move from the apparently "disjointed features" and "incoherent altitudes" which first greet the eye to a "solid network of true relationships" which harmonizes that incoherent disjointedness into a satisfying "unity" of aspect (VP 45/66–67). The Duhemian flavor is unmistakable.

The "majority of scientists," he admits, "do not even think of proclaiming this postulate"; but the reason for that, he suggests, is simply that it has become so "evident" and "habitual" to them. Teilhard's pro-scientific bias may have persuaded him to give more credit to his fellow-scientists than later events will justify: he may have been more accurate in admitting, to the readers of *Etudes*, that there might be sympathizers with the evolutionary theory who could not always "explain," even to themselves, the "reasons" for their sympathies (VP 7/18). Not everyone is equally aware of what is implied by their "habitual" way of doing, or seeing, things. But bring those habitual implicits to the surface, Teilhard is convinced, and it will become clear as day that in order to understand why any particular atom or molecule occurs at this rather than some other "place" in the evolving universe, the explanation must bear in mind no less than the "immensity of a whole astral evolution" (VP 101/141). Even when attending to the most elementary particle of scientific analysis, therefore, the scientist precisely as scientist must keep peripherally in mind the cosmic "whole," with whose every other item it interrelates.

Two closing comments are in order concerning Teilhard's notion of seeing with an "educated eye": (*a*) that he seems clearly to have been influenced by the landmark essay on "The Eyes of Faith," written by his friend Father Pierre Rousselot; and (*b*) that his confidence in the "educated eye" is very much the confidence of a geologist-paleontologist.

Pierre Rousselot was a fellow-Jesuit, one of Teilhard's companions during the first of his four years of theological studies at Hastings, and a friend he was obviously happy to rejoin in Paris. A powerful theological mind, Rousselot in 1910 published his famous essay on how the believer's "eyes" could see signs of God's working which escaped the eyes of others.[3] It soon caused a furor, for it was written at a time when "modernism" was likely to be charged against any adventurous theological proposal. More than likely Teilhard read it while at Hastings, and, as was his habit, discussed aspects of Rousselot's theory with the brilliant confrères who were to become his lifelong confidants on matters theological, Pierre Charles and Auguste Valensin. In any event, an explicit allusion to "the eyes of faith" in a letter written in January 1920 makes it clear that he was both familiar with and sympathetic to Rousselot's way of thinking.[4]

Capital to his thinking was the distinction between the believer's and the non-believer's *way* of "seeing." To introduce that distinction, Rousselot suggests that we consider how an experienced scientific researcher, or a seasoned detective "sees" what he sees. He brings to the process of looking for the solution latent in a tangle of evidence all the "experience" of dealing with similar problems in the past. But his knowledge from that past experience, while helping him enormously to "see" what someone less experienced could easily miss, does not function now in his work of detection as a body of knowledge which he consults, as it were, focusing on it to search for points of similarity with the problem currently confronting him; it has become part of his "habitual" *way* of looking at the evidence and for the solution: it is "perceptive, not perceived."[5] His very "eye" has been educated, by his accumulated experience,

---

[3] "Les Yeux de la foi," *Recherches des Sciences Religieuses,* 1 (1910), 241–59.

[4] See *Lettres intimes à Auguste Valensin, Bruno de Solages, Henri de Lubac, André Ravier, 1919–1925,* ed. Henri de Lubac, s.J. (Paris: Aubier–Montaigne, 1974), particularly the letter of January 10, 1920, p. 48, along with pp. 51–52n7.8. See also pp. 38, 68–69, 92. Directed to four theologians of mark, these letters go far to dispel any surviving notions one might entertain about Teilhard, the theological *naïf.*

[5] "Les Yeux de la foi," 251. Acting as *perceptive, non comme percue,* the researcher's knowledge is, in another of Rousselot's expressions, not an *avoir,* but a *habitus,* in the Thomist sense of a developed "power" of seeing in a specified way.

to *work* differently from the eye of one possessing less, or different sorts of, experience.

This, I submit, is evidently how Teilhard envisions the work of the scientifically "educated eye." To cite an analogous proposal from a more recent thinker: Michael Polanyi has stressed how much skillful activity, scientific or otherwise, depends on the functioning of the "tacit" dimension which enables us to see connections, for example, or to make instantaneous identifications, without focusing on the atoms of evidence and skeins of reasons which work behind the scenes, and always (necessarily) behind the scenes.[6] Obviously, too, there is a striking analogy here with Newman's "illative sense": both Rousselot and Teilhard are known to have been deeply interested in Newman's writings.[7]

But the "educated eye" to which Teilhard refers (and this he may have done so "tacitly" as to be unaware of the fact) was *primarily* that of the geologist-paleontologist. That was, after all, the kind of eye with which he was most familiar; hence, it was scarcely an accident that some of his richest early allusions to it are prompted by Suess's work on geology. Teilhard's specialty P. B. Medawar, in the classic rant which passed for his review of *The Phenomenon of Man*, has patronizingly termed a "comparatively . . . unexacting kind of science,"[8] but others will answer that charge better than I; at all events, to understand what kind of "eye" Teilhard is asking us to adopt, it is crucial to dwell for a moment on how the geologist-paleontologist "sees" the realities he explores.

Nothing could be luckier, to illustrate the workings of that kind of eye, than the publication of Carl Pantin's

---

[6] See his compact work *The Tacit Dimension* (Garden City, N.Y.: Doubleday, 1966), devoted to this facet of the earlier *Personal Knowledge: Towards a Post-Critical Philosophy* (Chicago: The University of Chicago Press, 1958; corrected edition, 1962).

[7] *Lettres intimes*, pp. 407–408.

[8] See pp. 101 and 105 of his review, cited in Introduction, note 2.

Tarner Lectures given at Trinity College, Cambridge University, in 1959. An eminent zoologist, but thoroughly innocent of any influence from either Teilhard or Rousselot, Pantin addressed himself to *The Relations Between the Sciences*.[9] The somewhat more usual but hackneyed divisions into descriptive and exact, observational and experimental, sciences, Pantin argues, do less than justice to the reality: he devises another distinction, between "restricted" sciences (like physics and chemistry) and "unrestricted" sciences (like biology and geology). The former, he notes, restrict themselves to a narrower range of phenomena, and need not consult their sister sciences in pursuing their explorations; the latter, on the contrary, range over a vaster field of phenomena, and must always be alert to the moment when physical or chemical analyses may become relevant to their investigations: they must "traverse" all the other scientific domains in pursuit of their own kind of findings. This, Pantin avers (*pace* Medawar), is why the unrestricted sciences are more, not less, demanding than physics and chemistry.

There is another difference between them: unrestricted sciences regularly deal with phenomena of larger size and/or duration than their restricted sisters;[10] Pantin gives the (geological) example of trying to understand the formation of an entire river-system.[11] This correlates, in part at least, with the consequence that the "experiments" of geology and biology occur far more frequently in "nature" than in the laboratory,[12] and with the further fact that a sort of total aesthetic recognition is more crucial in the unrestricted than in the restricted sciences: analyses of macro-phenomena down to their more and more minute component elements, along with exact mathematical measurements, although sometimes appropriate or even neces-

9 (Cambridge: Cambridge University Press, 1968).
10 Ibid., p. 20.
11 Ibid., pp. 9–13; see also pp. 153–54, 173–77.
12 Ibid., pp. 16–17.

sary, tend to take second place. The unrestricted scientist
may well return from the scene of his natural-site observation, sure of his findings there, but still feel obliged to set
down a list of analytic criteria, including mathematical
measurements when appropriate, then check them off, one
by one, in order to present to his confrères the "evidence"
for his conclusions. This is no purely formalistic exercise,
for "aesthetic" recognitions *can*, after all, involve such an
element of subjectivity that the scientist *may* end up seeing
what he wants to see; integrity and honesty, here, are all-
important. But granting integrity and honesty as part of
the scientist's equipment, he is always keenly aware that his
analytic procedures in the laboratory or museum seldom
if ever take in all he has observed; a considerable "residue"
from his initial observation leaks out, as it were, and never
gets conveyed in his analytic report. This compels him,
more often than not, to strive to communicate that "residue" by the use of striking similes or metaphors,[13] which he
knows his fellow-scientists, who have found themselves in
like situations, will interpret sympathetically as his effort
to pass on the total impression which in fact grounds his
conviction.[14]

Pantin concretizes all this by narrating the experience
of a particular geological "experiment." The problem involved explaining the historical formation of some Welsh
plateaux in the area of the river Towy. The first step in
solving it implied surveying the site, gaining that familiarity with its contours which only "field recognition" can
provide. Two hypotheses then presented themselves, each
of them, significantly, in conformity with the past experi-

---

[13] Ibid., pp. 84, 112–13. Pantin makes no apologies for this use of metaphor; it is standard form of communication in unrestricted science, and
particularly in geology. Again, the "languages" of science can be as legitimately diverse as the various sciences require. This point should be borne in
mind when considering Teilhard's resort to metaphor; it need not imply,
without further examination, that he is being poetical *rather than* scientific.

[14] Ibid., pp. 112–13; see also, on the scientific value of analogy, pp. 93–95.

ence of the American and English geologists, respectively, examining the site. Finally, O. T. Jones proposed that a closer study of the Towy, from its headwaters to the sea, might decide between the two competing hypotheses: this involved restudy of the site, and making exact measurements of the downward gradient that river followed on its journey toward the sea, a study which finally decided in favor of the theory Jones had proposed. Field recognition, hypothetical explanation of the features presented to that kind of "observation," but then, the discrimination between hypotheses by more "experimental" procedures involving exact measurements—this was the complete cycle of this piece of geological exploration.

But Pantin himself had only heard from other authorities of the theory which Jones had proposed; he found it, however, conformable with his own limited experience in geology. Nonetheless, he found that after learning of Jones's work he "immediately" began to view similar geological features in other parts of the world "with a different eye. It is not," he insists, "that I have the same perceptions as before and then apply Professor Jones's reasoning to them; it is as though my actual mode of perception has been changed by the historical experience of this argument." [15]

That education of the eye, of the very "machinery of perception" [16] itself, has several other implications as well. First of all, it suggests that terms like "observation" and "description" are deceptive even when applied to the geologist's very first steps toward "field recognition"; for the same tacit dimension which eventually works in the "recognition" stage is also at work before it. Secondly, it prompts the unrestricted scientist in choosing both time and place appropriate for crucial observation, as well as in actively

[15] Ibid., p. 13; see also note 11, above, for other loci where Pantin alludes to this same "experiment."

[16] Ibid., p. 17; the echo of Rousselot's *perceptive, non percue* is striking.

selecting out those of the innumerable phenomena before him which his past experience and theoretical "templates" cue him into knowing as relevant to the problem he is working with.[17] Of particular concern to the geologist, of course, is his choice of appropriate observation points, of what Teilhard calls privileged "points of vantage" (PM 32–33/ 26–27) from which the landscape "lights up," as it were, and the geologist "sees" how the work of ages went into producing this mountain range, this moraine, these intersecting valleys.

But this habit of educated vision is of special importance to the geologist, more so perhaps than to any other scientist; hence, one may guess, Teilhard's outspoken predilection for it as the metaphor for all scientific knowing. George Barbour and Helmut de Terra, two fellow-scientists who traveled with him on lengthy field expeditions, were especially struck by Teilhard's powers of vision: from the acuteness of sheer eyesight (but educated eyesight) which could spot from yards away a primitive tool lying in what his professional peers saw as only a pile of pebbles, up through the ease with which he saw the Himalayas through his experience of Egypt and the Alps, to the "inner eye" which unhesitatingly glimpsed the evolutionary meaning encased in a fossil tooth or a mountain upthrust.[18] Literally, as de Terra puts it, his "eyes were everywhere." But this heightened power to "see" may ironically have worked to his ultimate disadvantage: like an accomplished golfer who cannot empathetically understand why the game is so difficult for others, he may have been led to underestimate the task of educating eyes, even scientific eyes, whose "tacit dimensions" were far less or otherwise equipped than his own.

[17] Ibid.

[18] See Barbour's *In the Field with Teilhard de Chardin* (New York: Herder & Herder, 1965), p. 35; and de Terra's *Memories of Teilhard de Chardin*, trans. J. Maxwell Brownjohn (New York: Harper & Row, 1964), pp. 36–39, 62, 67, 72.

For Teilhard's scientific "eyes" were, again, very much those of a geologist-paleontologist. That must be kept in mind when we encounter two further particularities of his thinking: his use of the term "experimental," and the ease with which he deals with that scientific bogeyman, "anthropomorphism."

The French term *expériment* has as its corresponding adjective the term *expérimental*. The terms have a wider extension than their cognates in English, which permits of a distinction between properties which can be dealt with by "experimental" method in the strict sense and those which can be "experienced" in the more everyday sense of that term. The situation is complicated by the fact that "experiment," for the English scientific reader, more often suggests the style and standards of the "laboratory" experiment practiced by physicists and chemists.

But the French term *expérimental* stretches wider than that; it includes any and all phenomenal properties which can be "experienced," even if they are not of the sort which can be verified or tested by scientific "experiment" on the physical model. Teilhard's use of the term is influenced not only by the breadth of denotation it enjoys in French, but also by the kinds of "experimental" observations the geologist-paleontologist is accustomed to making "in the field" rather than in the museum or laboratory. So he will later feel entitled to say that "psychic" properties like thought, groping, invention, and the rest are just as "experimental," just as accessible to verification by observation, as physical properties like weight, mass, velocity, or radiation. The scientist whose model is physics will be tempted to quarrel with that contention, but Teilhard had exorcised early on any lurking adoration he may once have had of physics as the very model and norm for the way scientific activity was supposed to be conducted.

But talk of thought, groping, and invention as scientifically "experimental" properties would tend to alienate the physicist and chemist for an additional reason. Are these properties observable—experienced, even if not "experimentally" verifiable—on the human level? Some "experimental" scientists would concede it, but others, even psychologists like B. F. Skinner, would flatly deny it.[19] In any event, the question need not interest them greatly as *practicing scientists*, for the reason that physics and chemistry have long since come tacitly to agree that no such "anthropomorphic" properties may be invoked as operative on the physical and chemical levels of reality. The history of this decision on the part of post-Renaissance science to eschew all "anthropomorphism" is an interesting one; particularly fascinating is the way it has been transformed, in the minds of many scientists, from a methodological *abstraction* eschewing appeal to any such properties to a dogmatic *negation* that any such properties either exist or can be known to exist.

But the paleontologist is something of an oddity in this respect: not only must he constantly appeal to anthropomorphic forms of thought; one might even say they are his stock in trade, essential to the precise business he is about. For one of the most frequent questions he is called upon to answer is whether this or that fossil find is a "human" find, and to answer such questions he must avail himself of what he knows about human beings: that they make tools, use fire, invent not only material instruments but rites, languages, cultures. Thought, groping, invention: he moves at ease with the evidence he finds for the presence and operation of such "psychic" properties; indeed, he could not do otherwise. And in doing so, he never for a moment doubts the "scientific" character of the evidence he deals with, or of the methods he brings to dealing with

---

[19] Skinner's *Beyond Freedom and Dignity* (New York: Knopf, 1971) is a perfect illustration of this. See, for starters, pp. 1–23, where Skinner lays out his overall program—one based, be it noted, on the hopes he shares (with Duhem, and with Teilhard) for a comprehensive and unitary science.

it. "Experimental" evidence and method, one might query? The answer comes, especially when the question is asked in French, in an unhesitating "yes."

But even while Teilhard was penning the lines we have just examined, there was another aspect of scientific procedure which was rising to the level of his reflective awareness. He is beginning to grasp more focally the implications of the fact that the evolutionary cosmic "whole" constitutes the stuff of "history." Already implicit in everything he has written thus far, that historical dimension, once focused on, will prompt a series of proposals which his fellow-scientists will find, as time goes on, profoundly unsettling.

4

Science as History
and
Product of History

ONE OF THE MOST PIVOTAL ESSAYS Teilhard wrote, in gradually developing the method he eventually brought to writing *The Phenomenon of Man*, appeared in the review *Scientia* in 1925. It bears the title: "The Natural History of the World" (VP 103–13/143–57).

He starts from the attempts of Linnaeus and others to furnish a "systematics" aimed at presenting the "natural distribution" of living beings into classes and subclasses. Working, as they had to, with no idea that the assemblage of living forms was the result of evolutionary history, they thought of their divisions and subdivisions as corresponding, presumably, to the divine creative ideas presiding over the creation of a fixist universe. This obliged them, Teilhard explains, to apply a certain number of "extrinsic" criteria born of the play of their ordering intelligence; the result was that their divisions in many instances remained merely "logical" and to that extent artificial. Only when these life forms could finally be placed in *historical* sequence, the ordering mind placing each form and the entire assemblage in a "physical system" involving both "temporal antecedents" and "spatial links," could this logical and partially artificial system of classification yield to what Duhem had years ago proclaimed to be the ideal of scientific activity, a "natural classification" (VP 103–104/ 145–46).[1]

[1] Note the express correspondence between natural "distribution" and natural "classification," and compare chap. 2, note 6, above.

The evolutionary perspective not only permits, but now obliges, the "natural historian" to be more historian than ever; he not only must account for the geographical distribution, biological environment, and family relationships among various life forms, but must do so by presenting the "organic history" of each of those forms, attaching each to some evolutionary "prototype" and at the same time showing forth its connections with its "neighboring forms." Furthermore, the task of contemporary "systematics" involves no less than assigning each form its "true, natural place" in the entire "assemblage" of living forms; that task it cannot execute successfully unless it view that entire assemblage as "a whole," and, indeed, an "organized" whole, one enmeshed in a "process of development." No single living species can any longer remain intelligible to the scientific mind unless account be taken of the "place it holds by birth in the whole edifice of organized forms."

The evolutionary perspective implies, therefore, that each relic in the natural historian's museum must be assigned not only a "place," but also a "time" which answers perfectly to that place; everything must henceforth be situated in the unitary matrix of "space–time." But also implied is the requirement that the space–time situation of any single item take into account the space–time development of the "whole."

Again, no moderately reflective scientist would have any quarrel with these proposals, except perhaps to balk at the implication that the assemblage of living forms constitutes not merely a "whole" but an "organized" whole. We shall have to come, farther on, to Teilhard's justification of that term; at the moment, he is concentrating on drawing out another consequence of these reflections on "history." For they affect more than the biological science of "systematics." The evolutionary perspective, and the fundamental unity and set of interrelationships which it implies, affect not only the realm of living forms, but the "realm of matter" itself; the moment humans achieved an insight into the space–time development of living forms, "zoology and botany" became, not sciences separated off from, but "part of the block already formed by . . . physics, chemistry, and astronomy" (VP 104/146). For evolution obliges the zoologist, for example, seriously to consider whether the mutations he studies are not themselves a "function of the physico-chemical conditions regulating the *astral* evolution of the earth as a whole," and so to see his science as intimately connected not only with physics, chemistry, and astronomy, but geophysics and geochemistry as well. But the converse is also true. The physicist, chemist, and astronomer are by the same reasoning solicited to view their disciplines as contributing to the same "natural history" as concerns the zoologist: as erecting a "vast systematics of the inorganic world," a systematics which will be called upon, in time, to situate the various "atomic groups" it studies as space–time products of a "sidereal evolution." Eventually, we may be speaking not only of the "tree of life" but of a "tree of inorganic units" both atomic and sidereal: an older tree and more primordial, but already beginning to "relay with its branches" the tree of life (VP 112/156–57). In short, where we once were content to see the various "sciences" as distinct, the advent and triumph of evolutionary views brings us "closer every day" to the "fusion" of these various disciplines (VP 104/146). For we can now see what they have been doing all this while, as unconsciously as the pre-evolutionary exponents of "systematics," perhaps, but just as really. Each science has been studying some form which the cosmos has assumed in the successive phases of its evolution; now all of them have become aware of the space–time interrelationships linking those various forms. It is inevitable, Teilhard is convinced, that the pressure of this insight will compel

in the temporal series is to ask of him what the "perceptual laws" which preside over his entire way of investigating reality simply forbid him to furnish, or even to entertain as a scientifically discoverable possibility!

Here again, Teilhard's intention seems clearly that of "defending science" against anti-evolutionary theologians and philosophers who would require the scientist to admit to some such "absolute beginning." They must be brought to understand why, for the scientist *qua* scientist, they are asking for a self-contradiction; asking him to find some object in the time series "without *any* antecedent" in that time series is like asking him to locate an object in space "with no neighbor" whatever (VP 131–32/184). Can astronomy, for instance, ever discover the "beginning" in which God "created heaven and earth," or paleontology uncover evidence for a "first" man and woman, first because they, or at least their human "souls," were immediately created by God? If so, science would have discovered some reality which had been "born" but not "from what existed before" it. That the very laws of scientific perception make it impossible for science ever to accomplish.

But there is a caution here for the scientist as well: that no matter how far we push our "experience of the perceptible, we cannot but remain in the perceptible." The anti-evolutionist may be misguided in asking the scientist to locate an absolute beginning which would furnish a kind of "fissure" in the perceptible through which we might "pierce the veil of phenomena" and "look beyond appearances." This the scientist is unable to do precisely because the world he explores, the perceptual world, is constructed in such a way as to make our "perceptions the absolute prisoners of its immensity," and the scientist *qua* scientist must recognize the limits imposed by that bondage. But this implies realizing that his method eschews the further task of offering an "explanation of things," whether "of their external form or, even less, of the reason for their existence."

The scientist puts the philosopher on notice that it would hereafter be "useless" to present any account for the elementary units in our world "in isolation from the whole," but beyond that, he provides the philosopher with no "new access to the hidden level of structures and causes." The "absence of all empirical beginnings" does not entail a universe "invested with divine attributes"—the "unbounded" character of the universe as perceptual "has nothing to do with infinity" in the philosophical sense of that term—nor does "the fact that our mind does not perceive any first link in the chain of phenomena" entitle us to conclude to "the non-existence of an ontological beginning of duration" (VP 131n1/184n1). "Far from tending to discover a new God, science only goes on showing us matter," inviting our minds to voyage with it farther and farther down interminable reaches of cosmic time. But that voyage through time can never arrive at eternity: "One approaches the Absolute, not by traveling, but by ecstasy" (VP 132/185).[2] Science is barred by the very laws of its operations from saying anything about what that "ecstasy" might succeed in glimpsing.

Even these final remarks, Teilhard could feel confident, any scientist who had reflected on the implicits of his method would have little difficulty understanding and accept-

---

[2] I do not mean to discuss here the way Teilhard deals (VP 132–42/185–97) with the theological and metaphysical implicits of his adversaries' case. He argues for a notion of continuous creation wherein God never ceases to "make things make themselves," a creation whose phenomenal effect would be the evolutionary universe of our experience. He insists that the creative power must be conceived of, not as temporally intruding itself into, but rather as sustaining, the entire spatio-temporal network of secondary causes; and he contends that a mankind emerging from the entire panorama of cosmic history would be a mankind no less specially, but even more uniquely, "willed" by the creator. Suffice it to say that on most of these issues Teilhard may well have shown himself a considerably stronger theologian and metaphysician than his attackers seem to have been. These questions, though, pertain to that larger Teilhardian dialectic referred to in note 11 of the Introduction to this study. The validity of that larger dialectic, however, depends importantly on the validity of the way Teilhard built up his "vision of the past": that is my limited concern in these pages.

ing. But he intimates another conclusion as well. "Systematics" as a science has "evolved" under the pressure of the evolutionary insight. Systematics *has* a history, and its history has compelled it to "become" history in the fullest sense. But why should this happen only to systematics: why should one not anticipate a similar historical fate for her sister sciences? Each of them has a history, surely, and for each of them, that history began in pre-evolutionary days. What guarantee do we have that "doing" physics, or chemistry, or astronomy, will mean the same thing fifty years from now as it does today?

But the "alliance" of sciences to which Teilhard looks forward may be one thing; a "fusion" of sciences suggests quite another. How does Teilhard envisage the way astronomy, or biochemistry, will go about its business in the future? Some, at this point, may be tempted to conjecture that he would have all the sciences melt into a kind of poetic effusion or mystical rapture. But the sobriety of his proposals up to now suggests it might be fairer to hear him out.

5

Science, "Hypothesis," and the Reality of Evolution

SEVERAL KEY ELEMENTS in Teilhard's approach to science, its method, and its relationship with philosophy (as well as theology) advertise convincingly his enduring indebtedness to the Pierre Duhem who had guided his earliest steps onto this slippery terrain. The aim of science remains that of furnishing a "natural classification" of the laws and theories—and realities—it attempts to order in a way that satisfies the mind. But scientific explanation differs from philosophic explanation; it remains ineradicably on the level of phenomena, and refuses to have anything to say about the more "hidden causes" which are the legitimate concern of philosophic explanation. The quarrels between theologians and philosophers, on the one hand, and evolutionary scientists, on the other, would largely cease to be if those distinctions were more clearly borne in mind.

Duhem's influence becomes even more manifest when Teilhard confronts the objection that evolution is merely a "hypothesis," the implication being that, like so many former scientific hypotheses, it would more than likely "strut and fret its hour upon the stage" but then, its heyday passed, be quietly consigned to the garbage heap. This, we know, was the constant refrain among the most authorized (and authoritarian) representatives of Roman theology.

"Hypothesis," Teilhard will exclaim in an essay written later (1939), is a "very unsuitable word for the supreme spiritual act by which the dust of experiment assumes form and life in the fire of knowledge." But despite the poetic enthusiasm, he remains in firm control of how the mind moves in this "synthetic" phase of scientific creativity. There is, he proposes, a twofold criterion operative when we search for a pattern—Duhem's "natural classification" spontaneously comes to mind—to "fit" the welter of evidence amassed by "experimental" investigations.[1] The first of them is "coherence." One is initially "arrested" by some "general vision" which might make sense of that evidence; one stares, as it were, through the lens of that vision, and slowly it "begins, without forcing or distortion, to fit together the items it is bringing into order." Intelligence is active, but at the same time "obedient" to the contours of the evidence, in its search (Duhem would say) for a classification which is "natural," not forced or artificial. But there is a second criterion as well, indissolubly connected with the first: "fertility." From the "grouping" arrived at in the first step, there floods in upon the mind a new power of "comprehending" the evidence; at the same instant our "action" is enhanced by an increased power of "construction." The "coherence" of a natural classification inevitably entails successful pragmatic results; here, Teilhard

---

[1] "The Natural Units of Humanity," originally published in *Etudes* in 1939, is reprinted in VP (192–215/271–301). The explanation of "hypothesis" occurs on 205–206/289–90. In *Teilhard's Mysticism of Knowing*, King alludes several times to this quotation in a way which suggests that it has mystical implications, but the context shows that Teilhard is speaking, albeit enthusiastically and a trifle poetically, of hypothesizing in the sense in which a creative scientist would recognize that activity.

The mention of the "dust of experiment" makes it clear that the "coherence and homogeneity" which Teilhard frequently offers as hallmarks of a successful theory are meant as features of a theory constantly at grips with "the facts"—just as Duhem would have it. These "logical" properties of a theory are necessary, but not in themselves sufficient to warrant our confidence that the classification they characterize is "natural," i.e., reflecting genuine ontological relationships in reality. Teilhard, I am convinced, would have been bemused at the accusation that he was arguing for a pure "coherence" theory of scientific truth.

submits, we have the twin touchstones of "truth" (VP 205–206/289–90).[2]

Understood this way, he writes in 1925, hypothesis is not only the "aim," but the very "soul and true content of scientific theory," not merely (as so often understood) some "provisional and transitory means" of bringing order into our knowledge (VP 112n1/156n1). Some recent philosophers, Teilhard admits, have stressed the "precarious life" which hypotheses have been known to enjoy in the history of science; they have brought us to see, for instance, the "simplifications, approximations, and interpretations" which the "facts" of "concrete nature" undergo when dealt with in terms of mathematical laws—the very issues Teilhard himself was forced to confront in writing his earliest essay on this topic. All this has persuaded those thinkers to lay stress on the "relative and provisional character of human knowledge, especially in physics"—and to give the impression that whatever its practical efficiency might be, science is powerless to extend our "perception of reality" and to construct a "gradually more intelligible universe" (VP 110/154).

Again, Teilhard swings over to a defense of science; there is a good part of exaggeration in these "criticisms." And his reasoning remains faithful to the suggestions made

[2] It would be worth researching whether events in the meantime persuaded Teilhard to place this greater emphasis on the "pragmatic" character of any good hypothesis than he formerly had. It is fair to say, however, that the pragmatic notion was far from absent in Duhem; see his *Aim and Structure*, trans. Wiener, pp. 27–30, a section Teilhard almost surely read in the original article in the *Revue de Philosophie* (compare the citations in chap. 1, notes 6–19, above, and see *War Writings* 162/184). This pragmatic emphasis, however, only accents the realist and "fact-anchored" cast of Teilhard's scientific thinking from start to finish; it also raises questions about how that realism ultimately coheres with the "idealism" for which King, *Teilhard's Mysticism of Knowing*, pp. 54–56, suasively argues. We have a certain amount to learn here, but my present suspicion is that Teilhard was more attentive than King may have supposed to the "degrees of knowledge" he was dealing with, and dealing with differently because different contexts demanded it.

in that early essay: one must distinguish between the mathematical "expressions" and "representations" to which physics resorts, and the "physical entities" which its network of "laws and calculations" enable the physicist to discern and discover.[3] Those expressions and representations and their resulting mathematical "constructions" are unquestionably "relative," "idealized," and subject to changing styles in mathematical approach; mathematical laws, in short, are a "language" which could change its vocabulary and syntax tomorrow, but still "describe the same realities" as today. Take Leverrier's discovery of the planet Neptune as an example. We look upon the older astronomical laws and calculations he trusted in as merely "approximate" now; yet they brought him to hypothesize the existence of that previously unknown planet, and Neptune, once discovered, can never be undiscovered. It has passed forever from the status of a purely "hypothetical" entity to the physical reality we now know it to be. So too, the electron "hypothesis" was the result of earlier styles in mathematical physics, but proponents of more recent styles are not even tempted to deny the objective existence of electrons. The lesson should be clear: "Good hypotheses are continually modified," yes, but always "in a definite direction," the direction of increasing perfection. And in that process they leave behind a whole array of "definitive elements destined thereafter to feature in any scientific construct which would represent our world" (VP 112n1/156n1).

So, Teilhard is convinced, it has been with the evolutionary "hypothesis." It is chiefly the product of the new "systematics"; a science once content to furnish a "nominal or logical classification" of the life forms it studied, it has now taken a "new form" at the behest of a growing array of facts: the form of "history." That historical mode enables it to evince "new possibilities" as proof of its ongoing

---

[3] On the "language" analogy for scientific activity, compare Duhem in *Aim and Structure*, trans. Wiener, pp. 133, 151.

"fertility." But its "coherence" is proven by the way it has succeeded in detecting an "immense natural network of natural elements," in which "each newly discovered life form takes an effortless place, bringing additional completion to the continuity of the whole." Now the language becomes unmistakably Duhem's: *Everything is susceptible of classification; therefore everything holds together.* This "hypothesis" does not owe its existence to a "few isolated or fugitive facts"; nothing less than the "gigantic mass formed by the totality of living beings" has been arranged into the order of a "natural grouping" (VP 121/172; emphasis Teilhard's).[4] There is only one way of explaining the "structure of the life world discovered" by this new systematics: the only way we can "see it" correctly is by seeing it "as the result of a development, an 'evolution.' " This, Teilhard insists, is the "essential point"; whatever future modifications may affect the evolutionary hypothesis, and they may be many, we must not look for scientists of the future to change their minds on that essential point (VP 122/172). For once it is accepted, along with its implications, "reality is found to grow clearer and more orderly so far as the eye can see" (VP 104/147).

Besides its unmistakable "Duhemian" pedigree, there are two additional implicits of Teilhard's "defense" of science and its way of "seeing" the real which are worth remarking. Except for his increased stress on Duhem's original "pragmatic" criterion of "fertility," Teilhard's way of illustrating the "reality value" of the scientific view remains basically what it was in 1905; Duhem has proven a durable ally. The history of science warns us not to wed ourselves to this or that scientific "construction," or else

---

[4] Note, again, the implied correspondence between the logical properties of "classification" and the ontological relationships of a "natural grouping"; as usual, straight Duhem. So is the conclusion, which we shall have to consider farther on, that all this argues that the tree of life manifests no mere "chance association or accidental juxtaposition" but a "physically organized unity."

the succession of such constructions, each of relative value, will only plunge us into skepticism about science overall. Take each such construction as a "language," though, a language never to be understood in brutally literal terms, and the very succession of hypotheses becomes an argument *for* our continuing belief in science. But this implies that we remain constantly alert to the need for "translating" each member of that succession of scientific constructions, for peering *through* the parade of scientific models in order to espy the reality features to which they commonly point. Those reality features may vary, however; they can be existing entities, like electrons or the planet Neptune, but they can be "properties" of the real as well. Among those properties Teilhard mentions that reality presents itself to us as a "vast family of natural unities, centers, nuclei," their specific properties making them susceptible of being "grouped" (naturally, not artificially) "in graded categories (VP 112/156);[5] that living forms, specifically, all share a "physical and organic interdependence"; and that the universe boasts a "fundamental unity," all its "cosmic elements" being inexorably interrelated (VP 104/ 147). Those claims about the real may sound so vastly generalized as to be dreadfully minimal, but Teilhard is once again confident that anyone, scientist or non-scientist, who has followed his careful and necessarily qualified defense of science would see that the very minimal character of those claims puts his identification of those reality features as far beyond dispute as one can put it. Teilhard is one step nearer, now, to the technique he employs in *The Phenomenon of Man*: coaching his reader to discern what "imposed factors" the real itself must possess if we are to make sense of the historical truth that successive scientific constructs have each "worked" for their lifetime and passed the baton to their successors, leaving us in many cases with

[5] Again, on the "language" metaphor, see note 3, above.

irreversible and definitive findings of which every successor construct is constrained to take account.

There is, however, a second set of implicits, embedded in this "defense" of science and the evolutionary hypothesis. I have deliberately omitted them from the presentation of Teilhard's case just given. My reason for omitting them was this: the reality features which he has accented up to this point stand an excellent chance of being recognized and accepted by reflective scientists, but now Teilhard begins to point to an assemblage of other features which, many a scientist would more likely claim, are not nearly so evident—indeed, are highly questionable.

But first, one thing is common to most, if not all, the evolutionary characteristics to which Teilhard now turns our attention. He claims that they can be "seen" in the highly sophisticated meaning which that term has by now taken on in the course of his defense of science: but seen "through" the succession of models, as the "imposed factors" of the real which intelligence has arranged into a "natural" classification. The indispensable condition for achieving any such vision, however, is the familiar one: the scientist must consent to stand back from his analytic–regressive procedures for a long moment to take stock of the "whole," the totality of the perceptible world which *all* the sciences, in their half-acknowledged "alliance" with each other, have come—tacitly, for the most part—to read off as a single interconnected "history."

The necessity for taking this "middle distance" point of vantage was most vividly impressed on Teilhard, as we have seen, by Louis Vialleton's objections to the reality of evolution. In his answer to Vialleton, Teilhard implies that the evolutionary scientist does, in fact, take such "wholes" into account, and that his conviction that evolution actually took place depends upon his doing so, whether consciously or not. We are now about to turn to what else Teilhard claims is "seen" from this middle distance; but it should be kept in mind throughout that his allusion to these other features was thrust upon him by the necessities of arguing that evolution *did*, in fact, "happen."

Proving *that* evolution took place is one thing, Teilhard reminds Vialleton; the truth of this or that scientific construct aimed at explaining *how* it happened is quite another. An objection may be admitted as valid against this or that "how"-theory, without calling immediately into question *that* evolution did take place. This, we saw, was Teilhard's first line of defense in his answer to Vialleton. But later in that same essay, he is compelled to qualify that answer. Vialleton's objections were aimed at the very *possibility* of evolution's ever having happened, *if* one suppose that evolution necessarily operates "mechanistically." And, Teilhard seems in second-thought to have realized that, once evolution and mechanistic evolution are identified, Vialleton's objections could be viewed as bearing strongly against the very "fact" of evolution.

To Vialleton's objection drawn from the leaps and discontinuities in the fossil evidence, Teilhard replied—as he will consistently reply thereafter—that one must fully expect evolutionary "peduncles" to disappear. But Vialleton's two further objections could not be laid to rest so easily. He had pointed to the evidence that later life-forms "diverged" from the line of ideal development which the theory called for; and to the further evidence that, instead of showing up as developing forms, they appeared in the fossil record as "fixed" at a stage of (apparently) full development and wide distribution.

This appearance of fixity in forms which one would have expected to detect as fluid and moving, Teilhard takes as a serious objection, dubbing it the "paradox of transformism." But he admits that both fixity and "divergence" represent a kind of "twin mystery" (VP 90/127), and so, not surprisingly, his eventual reply to Vialleton must answer to both of them, taken as a single complex objection. First, however, he reminds Vialleton, the business of tracing the history of life forms *forward* may momentarily encounter difficulties; but the great point is what tracing forms *backward* in time reveals: that no later form ever occurs for which some earlier cannot be found, a less developed form which represents a kind of try-out "sketch" for its successor. Vialleton's own way of expressing himself betrays his implicit agreement on this point, and, Teilhard reasons, this inexorable law of "birth," succeeding forms from predecessors, suffices to establish the "physical" connection of life forms which is the essence of modern evolutionary theory (VP 88n1/125n1; cf. VP 84, 101/119–20, 141–42).

So much for the "fact" of evolution; can the "how" be explained in terms which elude the twin objections of fixity and divergence? Here, Teilhard avows, he must become more speculative. He bases those speculations largely on W. K. Gregory's studies of mutations, but extends Gregory's conclusions to propose a plausible way in which mutations could conceivably result in the discontinuities pointing to vanished peduncles, the sidewise leaps of divergence, and the appearance of fixity which those mutated populations all, as Vialleton had shown, assume in the fossil record (VP 90–92/128–30). Mutation theory was then in its infancy, and highly suspect to some evolutionists; but since Vialleton had contended that any such explanation was impossible, Teilhard may be thought to have won his point.

For the moment, at least. But in the course of winning it, he is compelled, first, to invite Vialleton to adjust his focus, and, secondly, to make some serious concessions on what mutation theory would imply.

The adjustment of focus he asks of Vialleton is one already familiar: to see that evolution "happened," he must enlarge his view to the whole history of life on earth. Before urging this larger view, however, Teilhard has taken a closer look at the way science more habitually goes about its task. Its more normal method is partly what makes its resulting views diverge from Vialleton's, and from those of many philosophers as well. Once again he explains that scientific method is dominantly analytic: it tends to explain everything by "taking it apart"; so, it tends to explain the constitution of any whole as the sum of its constitutive parts, and its functioning as the sum of the workings of those constituents. By the same token, however, scientific explanation, when placed in the space–time matrix, becomes regressive: it tends to explain later evolutionary phenomena in terms of the simpler and earlier elements which preceded, and from which the later "came forth" (VP 98/137–38).[6]

Again, Teilhard admits that the progress achieved by this analytic method has been no less than astonishing. The study of inanimate matter has brought us to the discovery of molecules and atoms, and put us on the track of more minute constituents still; the science of organic matter already reaches down to cells, protoplasm, cellular nuclei, and protein molecules, and promises to push the question farther yet, into territory previously thought to be the province of the chemist and physicist. Similarly, the study of things along the time scale follows the analytic process: the history of any being in our universe, once followed up, eventually leads to the same dissolution, the same disintegration into the elemental units of which it is composed.

If one imagines that this mode of explanation adequately "explains" the human being—to cite that important instance—one must then consent to admitting that the human is ultimately explained by its component atoms, the personal by the impersonal, the conscious by the unconscious, and freedom by determinisms (SC 27/53). Now, it was exactly Teilhard's contention that, even on the

[6] Compare also SC 24/49–50, written in 1921.

scientific level, this habit of explaining the functioning of a synthetic whole solely in terms of the action of its analytic parts was beginning to demonstrate its inadequacy. It was, as he puts it, becoming a serious question whether this kind of "atomism," despite its proven fruitfulness in the past, would much longer prove equal to the task of making reality "scientifically comprehensible." For alongside the properties of any "whole" which might be explained from the collective play of its component parts, every "organized whole" must possess other properties peculiar to the whole *as such*. Those holist properties, he was convinced, could never be accounted for by analyzing them down to, and thereupon adding up the sum of, the more "elementary forces" which analysis claimed to have uncovered (VP 98/ 137–38).

The point, we have seen, was not a new one for Teilhard; but Vialleton's objections had underlined its impor- tance, and summoned it into practical application in a new way. Vialleton had aimed a devastating series of objections at comparative anatomists who focused their study on the alleged development of one or other anatomical part, whether a paw, a limb, or a wing. The wing of speci- men "B" developed from the limb of specimen "A," they claimed; but they never alluded to, or perhaps even no- ticed, the difficulties which their claims encountered when the wing, on the one hand, and the limb, on the other, were viewed as functioning parts, coordinated with all the other functioning parts of the total animal to which they were respectively attached. It was, Vialleton objected, the abrupt recasting of the animal *as a whole* which begged for explanation, and the gradualism implied by mechanistic theories of evolution was utterly incapable of furnishing it.

Vialleton's point, Teilhard had to admit, was well taken; it served to show that biologists who persisted in the purely analytic approach were forgetting a lesson which the prog- ress of their science should by now have taught them: one cannot explain the transformation of the limbs and organs of any individual animal "without allowing for the power of heredity and coordination" which characterizes both the functioning, and the evolutionary mutation, of the animal precisely as a *whole* (VP 108–109/152). After any such "close-up" examination of this or that part, the scientist must step back in order to see whether his conclusions about any single part make sense in terms of what they imply about the whole.

Now, however, Teilhard asks Vialleton to be consistent with his own insight and to step back even farther; to see that life itself has a "history," one cannot limit oneself, as Vialleton has unwittingly done, to inspecting merely the "individuals" which constitute the "elementary components" of that historical stream. The stream itself is a "whole," though of another order. Examine a single droplet microscopically, and you lose sight of the movement of the stream; step back, and your attention may be caught by the minor eddies and countercurrents playing over the surface; step back even farther, and you lose clear sight of the droplets, and perhaps even of the eddies and countercurrents, but now at last you see a stream, flowing in a definite direction. The law can be generalized, and Teilhard, in time, will formulate it this way: "Nothing is perceptible in the world unless you position yourself at the 'spot' for looking at it." Collective entities can be "seen" but "only from a certain distance." They "show up" only when viewed in the "round," as all totalities must be viewed. Stand too close, and you cannot see them properly; but stand *too* far off, and once again, they can disappear (VP 198–99/281).

Now Teilhard responds to the need he sees of showing, even more clearly than before, that this view of "wholes" is already a recognized exigency in science. Not only active in the life sciences, it is not confined to them: radiation and spectrometric studies have led physical chemistry to concentrate on the evolution of cosmic matter viewed as a totality. Geology, he repeats his lesson from Suess, has been brought to invoke the notion of phenomena like "folds, overthrusts, continental distribution" and the like, which cannot be reduced to, or explained as, the mere sum of the activities of material entities "smaller in magnitude" than the earth itself. Geologists have come to see, accordingly, a class of "specifically terrestrial effects," proper to the unity called "earth"—as proper to the earth as other effects are proper to the unity "hydrogen atom" or to the unity "sun" (VP 109–10/153). Indeed, science in general seems to be maturing to the point of recognizing the need to study both "movements and unities" of no less than cosmic proportions (VP 110/153–54).

Much more clearly than before, Teilhard is persuaded he is not urging on science something entirely new; his familiarity with geological syntheses of the type which Suess had advanced has convinced him that the study of the "astral evolution of the earth," tending more and more to focus on our planet considered as a "specific whole," a whole as specific as any "chemical molecule," was fast becoming accepted scientific procedure (VP 106/149). But more pertinently, his analysis of how the life sciences implicitly arrive at the conviction that only the evolutionary hypothesis could account for the distribution of living forms has forced him even more explicitly to proclaim that such a conviction could never have been reached (or preached to its adversaries) unless the realm of life forms had been envisaged not only as a whole, but—and now he takes an important additional step—as an "organized" whole.

The clearest application of this mode of study was, in fact, to be found in the life sciences, and particularly in the branch most intimately connected with the study of living forms, "systematics." There, a whole array of phenomena forces the zoologist to entertain the idea of an interior "balance" within living groups considered as interacting and interdependent wholes, and, then, to take the further step of focusing on the "biosphere" entire as a single "organized mass" (VP 106–107). In acting this way, the zoologist has simply exploited Vialleton's own advice to the comparative anatomist: consider each living being holistically as a unitary complex of organs and functions, no one of which can be understood, scientifically, apart from its relationships to *all* the others, and to the total behavior of the unit-being itself.[7] So too the student of biospheric effects: every day it becomes plainer to him that each living group as such, and the biosphere entire, beg to be looked on as unified complexes of various subtypes, "carnivores, herbivores, swimmers, climbers, flyers, and burrowers," each subtype contributing in its way to the evolutionary viability of the group as a whole (VP 106/149).

The need for admitting such a total internal "balance" in a living group Teilhard finds warranted by the evidence attesting that "any fragment of life, sufficiently large," which for one reason or another becomes geographically isolated, tends to behave like a "cutting" shorn from the parent tree; eventually, it "reproduces as a stem the general design of the [entire] tree from which it was taken," including all the varied subtypes, from burrowers to flyers, from which it had been cut off (VP 99–138). The case of the Australian marsupials he finds particularly telling: the geological cataclysm which isolated Australia from the original continental mass resulted, not in the destruction of this curious group of living beings, but in the production of the whole variety of marsupials which we find there now, each subtype apparently contributing to the viability of the marsupials as a single mutually interrelated group (VP 16–17/29; cf. VP 85/121).

---

[7] This, we saw, was Vialleton's criticism of the standard "proofs" for evolution from comparative anatomy.

Another piece of evidence: mutations appear to occur, not in this or that individual, but "simultaneously in a relatively large number of individuals," with the result that an entire group begins to "drift" as a group in the same life direction (VP 99/139).

Finally, Teilhard proposes that "each new flowering of higher forms" appears to have the surprising effect of "lowering the pressure of the sap in the lower branches" of the evolutionary tree as a whole (VP 99/139).[8] Far from being arcane, he avers, such phenomena of interdependence are "well known" to scientists; whence the already long-standing discussions about the "life of species," the life of whole groups of living beings precisely as groups (VP 107–108/150–51). As "mysterious" as such phenomena may initially seem, they strongly suggest that "to interpret them, we must search for their center of action," not in this or that living individual, but in groups, and indeed in "life" taken as a whole (VP 100/139–40).

Science must not, in the old cliché, ignore the contours of the forest for having more and more minutely examined its individual trees. So, he points out, his fellow-geologists were so busy "counting the waves" or periodic geological changes that they almost failed to remark on the underlying movement of the "tide" (VP 46, 48/68, 69).[9] So too, the physicist: when he sets himself to studying the "form and spread of a wave," he instinctively focuses on some "isolated molecule" to catch its movement inside the movement of the entire wave; now, however, he is being solicited to shift from concentrating exclusively on the "pulsating molecule" to considering "the wave" itself (VP 195/276–

[8] One wonders how many scientists would agree that there is evidence (even in Teilhard's sense) for this large-scale estimate.

[9] Though taken from letters written well after the original publication of that article, these two applications of the "tide" metaphor accord perfectly well with the tenor of Teilhard's essay on "The Face of the Earth." Again, it is suggestive that Teilhard may well have transposed a metaphor from Duhem (see *Aim and Structure*, trans. Wiener, pp. 38–39), applying what is true of advancing science to the evolutionary advance which it studies.

77). This does not mean forgetting all we have learned by analytic study of the molecules; it calls for taking a larger, complementary view: "viewed through a microscope," the larger outlines of any macro-specimen "seem to vanish." But isn't this because the microscope is precisely the instrument most suitable for blurring those larger contours, even, at the extreme, making them "disappear from sight" (VP 198/280–81)?

With all of this, Teilhard must have expected Vialleton to be, at least in principle, sympathetic; it was, after all, a mere extension of his own advice to the comparative anatomist. Teilhard's stress on science's need synthetically to envisage wholes whose parts it had analyzed until now with much brilliant success will later bring him to put forth a number of observations on "how" evolution must have taken place; but, once again, it should be noted that he was first constrained to validate the strictly scientific need for such "middle distance" vision in the interests of explaining why and how he, along with his scientific fellows, came to be so firmly convinced *that* evolution *did* take place.

But Vialleton has forced him to realize, perhaps more clearly than heretofore, that these two questions might not be so cleanly divorceable after all. For Vialleton's objections were sharply aimed at showing that mechanistic forms of evolutionary theory set up certain expectations concerning how the fossil evidence should "line up" in order to substantiate their claim that life, including human life, was from bottom to top the product of an evolution: the fossils should, on this hypothesis, fall along relatively simple, almost straight lines of continuous and gradual development. And since mechanism must postulate just such a gradual, continuous development, the fossils should testify to life forms, not stable and to all appearances fixed, but fluid, rather, plastic, and in evolutionary "movement." Evolutionary theorists, Vialleton charged (with some embarrassing instances which supported his charge), too often presented the factual evidence in such "idealized" form, both partial and partisan, as to create the "illusion" of transformism instead of proving that it ever truly happened—and, *sub voce*, happened *the way* their theory must postulate it happened.

Now, Teilhard makes it clear that he holds no brief for "tricking out" the fossil evidence, where and whenever that may have occurred.[10] But the "idealization" of the "factual" evidence, he sees, need not amount to its falsification. Here he recognizes an analogy to the charge against mathematical physics with which he had concerned himself in his earliest essay: not only physics, he is persuaded, but science more generally always idealizes the roughage of experimental approximations with which observation furnishes it. It never happens that all the factual data fall uniformly along the ideal graph-line of theoretical expectation. But instead of charging that science is not interested in dealing with facts, Teilhard's entire strategy in defending scientific "realism" consisted in remaining constantly aware of *how* the succession of scientific theories could illumine us on the "imposed factors" of the real. So, in a brief but pregnant aside (whose force he obviously expects Vialleton to appreciate), he calmly admits that the graph of evolutionary sequences traced by contemporary theorists represents only a kind of "ideal axis" which in fact "zigzags" its way through the "real" sheaf of fossil specimens (VP 89/126–

---

[10] On the bizarre fantasy that Teilhard was guilty of just such a "hoax" in the Piltdown case, see Mary Lukas, "Teilhard and the Piltdown 'Hoax,'" *America*, 144, No. 20 (May 23, 1981), 424–27. Jacques Monod, *Chance and Necessity*, pp. 31–33, accuses Teilhard of that intellectual "spinelessness" and compromising "truckling" which one should only expect from a man whose religious order Pascal long ago found guilty of "theological laxness." Poor stuff, that, reflecting more on Monod than on Teilhard.

27). Everyone acknowledges that the real is more complicated than earlier theorists anticipated it would turn out;
but isn't this always the way with science?

But the expectations set up by earlier evolutionary theorists were, he grants Vialleton, simpler and cleaner than
later-found evidence sits well with. And part of the problem with those earlier theoretical expectations was, he must
now admit, the mechanistic "way" they set about proving
"how" evolution must have occurred. But those clean-
limbed mechanistic expectations must be acknowledged a
thing of the past, one more relic of an epoch when to "be
scientific" meant to ape as closely as possible the "noblest"
of sciences, mathematical physics, with its apparent, but
deceptive, appanage of mechanistic determinism. The expectations of contemporary evolutionists have shifted into
a more biological key, and those biological expectations
are precisely those which more recent fossil finds tend more
and more to confirm.

Once again, the most decisive path through the fossil
remains runs *backward* in time, from the more fully developed forms to the earlier "sketches" which Vialleton
himself implicitly recognizes: the "fact" of evolution reposes in the first instance on this universal law of "birth"
and on the "physical" connection it discloses running
through the history of life on our planet. But to answer
Vialleton completely, evolutionary theory must now face
the challenge of taking a second "forward" path as well:
the law of birth implies as its corollary a coordinate law
of "growth."

So, Teilhard was brought to see, one may not, when all
is said, elude the challenge of showing that the fossil evidence convincingly argues that life, in all its various forms,
"grew" upon our planet. In confronting that challenge,
though, he must remain substantially faithful to the ground
rules his defense of scientific realism has laid down. First,
he is obliged to envisage life as a single "natural history,"

moving from primeval cosmic matter through plant and animal forms, and not excluding the emergence and history of humanity. Secondly, he must show that envisioning life as this historical growth enables us to uncover a "natural" classification for everything from hydrogen to humanity. At this point, the twin questions touching *whether* and *how* evolution happened fuse into one: because proving that evolution permits us to find a "natural classification" now involves proving, at a single stroke, *that* it happened precisely because this "how" of its happening makes sense— simply, effortlessly, without forcing it or doing it violence —of the factual evidence. And, thirdly, Teilhard must accomplish all this without wedding himself irrevocably to any *particular*, and conceivably transitory, "theory" of evolution, be it Darwinian, Lamarckian, or whatever. He must carefully confine his appeal to those "imposed factors" of the real which commonly underlie all such "valid" theories as they relay each other in ever-increasing precision.

In executing this exacting mandate, Teilhard appeals to a variety of models or analogies. Any scientific model, after all, begins as a suggestive analogy. Virtually all of them have this in common: they jog our minds into seeing "wholes."

Evolution implies "movement." The analogy of the "stream" warns us against focusing exclusively on droplets, eddies, secondary countercurrents; the stream, precisely as a stream moving in a definite direction, can be seen only at a certain "distance."

But evolution most crucially implies "growth," the kind of growth we recognize as *genuine* growth. Here Teilhard draws his analogies from instances where, scientists or no, we recognize growth as an unquestionable reality: a tree, a bush, an animal. But what, in these examples, entitles us to point to growth as genuine? We may not have reflected on it, but Vialleton's objections now oblige us to do so. No animal, to start there, is simply an assemblage of anatomical parts and organs, slapped together anyway, anyhow. The animal is a living *unit*, its parts and their functioning all interrelated, interdependent, coordinated; it is, in a word, an "organized" unity of functioning parts. Alter (by mutation, if you will) any single part, and for the animal to function viably, all other parts must be altered in some corresponding way. The terms of this, Vialleton's objection to the anatomical "proofs" for evolution, Teilhard accepts but only to turn against him.

A similar organization can be detected in the "tree"; its limbs and branches radiate outward and upward from the trunk in the coordinated interdependence necessary for the survival and growth of the tree as a single living unit. But, the objection might be raised, the analogy of the "tree of life" is too neat and orderly to fit the tangle which the accumulating fossil evidence confronts us with. In that case, Teilhard replies, change the analogy to that of a "bush"; but even in that case, the properties of unity, interdependence, "organization," while faintly obscured, remain ineffaceably there.

But natural history embraces human history as well. Humanity too is the product of evolutionary growth, a growth which began with the movements of cosmic matter in its least developed forms. This fundamental continuity of primitive matter, the varied forms of living beings, and humanity grounds Teilhard's assurance that analogies drawn from the human sphere may also, quite legitimately, furnish "models" to illumine evolution's ways of growth. So, in proposing his reflections on "mutation" theory, he stresses that mutations would entail the stops, starts, sideways leaps, the long periods of fixity on which Vialleton directed his fire. But these, Teilhard points out, are the very properties of evolutionary "growth" which one uncovers in the development of human societies and civilizations; it should be no surprise, in fact one should have expected, to find them already manifest, on a more rudimentary level, in the earlier phases of the same process which eventually produced those societies and civilizations (VP 97, 68–71/ 136, 98–101).[11]

It might be objected that Teilhard has been brought to stress the "organized" character of evolutionary products out of some unavowed "apologetic" intent: that he meant to read these properties *into* evolution in the hope of making the theory more palatable for Catholic adversaries like Vialleton. That objection might seem to gather strength when we come to study the implications which he began to draw, even in this essay, for understanding the "how" of evolution, implications which he saw as flowing necessarily from its "organizing" character. However one is inclined to reply to such imputations of sinister intent, this much ought to be acknowledged: Teilhard's original stress on "organization," interrelatedness, and coordinated interdependence was forced upon him by the logic of the argument he was conducting to prove *that* evolution did actually occur. His claim was that evolutionary theory, as against the anti-evolutionary constructs favored by its adversaries, provided a "natural" rather than artificial or merely logical classification of the fossil evidence. The implication is that evolutionary theory puts the scientist's inquiring mind in "resonance," so to speak, with the "way nature itself works," with the way we would expect a world of growth to "look" if it did, in fact, *physically* "grow." It was because Vialleton had forced the issue, making it ineluctable to acknowledge the properties of organization as characteristic of growth, that Teilhard was logically compelled to appeal to those features disclosing "how" evolution occurred in order to demonstrate that what *did* occur actually was, and had to be, an "evolution." It was, after all, at least conceivable that the various strata of fossils, each more de-

[11] Alluded to at first only in passing, this insight is then developed in the later "Hominization" essay.

veloped than the other, *could* have resulted from God's successive creative interventions, guided by some design of what an "ideal" assemblage of living forms would look like, once His final creative intervention had taken place. These successive creations of stable forms would then result in a "simulated," but non-actual, evolution. Teilhard implies that some such notion was Vialleton's only alternative to evolutionary theory (VP 102n1/142n1);[12] it contained, he argued, difficulties both theological and philosophical (VP 24–25/38–39);[13] but his principal fire is directed at the wreckage it makes of all our scientific knowledge. The "organized" character of evolutionary growth permits of a "natural classification"; that natural classification rhymes with the way our minds would expect nature to work, producing an assemblage of living forms whose interconnections were genuinely *physical* (VP 121–22/171–72).[14] Object that these connections may be merely "simulations," and the achievement of a natural classification no longer warrants the scientist's confidence that he has come to some knowledge of the real, and the entire edifice of scientific endeavor has been reduced to a shambles. Scientists who would insist on claiming that evolution actually occurred, but in a random, haphazard way, have simply failed to take the measure of this problem, Teilhard is convinced; and he is determined to do nothing less than "save science."

The importance of "organization" for proving the factual character of evolution is even more peremptorily stressed in an unpublished essay dating from two years later, in 1926.[15] Here, moreover, Teilhard's argumentative intention in appealing to this characteristic of the evolu-

[12] See the argument, in more developed form, in VP 24–25/38–39.

[13] See above, Introduction, note 11, and chap. 4, note 2.

[14] To the claim that this "whole" must explicitly be recognized as an "organized" one, we shall come shortly.

[15] "The Basis and Foundations of the Idea of Evolution" remained unpublished until its inclusion in VP (116–42/163–97).

tionary process is clear beyond doubt. The most "general" —indeed, the "unique and inexhaustible"—proof that organized matter actually evolved is to be found in the evidence of "structure" which the world of life forms discloses when contemplated as a "whole." That world evinces the existence of "vast animated complexes" constituting so many "natural distributions" whose inter-linkings can be seen as clearly as the "relation of parts interior to each plant or animal viewed in isolation" (VP 116–17/165– 66).[16] The entire opening section of this essay is devoted to proving that evolution actually happened. The clinching proof is drawn from the observation that the members of this "totality of living beings" were neither "associated by chance" nor "accidentally juxtaposed"; they constitute, rather, an "ensemble which is physically organized," a "*constructed whole.*" The "conclusion" follows: it "took shape progressively"; it can only have been the "result of a development, an 'evolution' " (VP 121–22/172); it "was born" and it "grew" (VP 122/173).

But, Teilhard must admit, the tack he has taken in defending the reality of evolution against Vialleton's objections may bring him into disfavor with his fellow-scientists. For one thing, his interpretation of mutation theory, however provisionally offered, implies that science take note of properties in the real, and adopt a kind of thinking about them, which it has hitherto considered anathema. These reflections may strike the scientist as smacking, first of all, of an outmoded "vitalism"; against that charge, Teilhard mounts a careful argument in his own defense.[17] But, ad-

[16] These are the introductory portions of the essay referred to in note 15, above.

[17] "Vitalism" means various things to various scientists, often depending on their differing grasp of the philosophical issues involved. Teilhard makes quite plain (VP 95–97/134–35), first, what he means by a vitalism which no scientist should feel obliged to accept, and, then, how his proposal differs from any such objectionable view. The pivotal point consists in conceiving of "life" not as "intercalated" as one more among the series of physico-chemical causes at work, then postulating that it boasts some special "measurable" effect of

ditionally, he is asking the scientist resolutely to recognize and to take account of the "psychic" factors which the paleontologist habitually deals with in his explorations of primitive humanity. Nothing very scandalous there, one might reply—except that Teilhard is asking that the presence and activity of those psychic factors, including a kind of instinctive "inventiveness," be recognized as playing a role in the organic transformations which science uncovers in the *sub*human world.

How receptive Vialleton might be to such suggestions Teilhard must only guess; but he himself has reached a point in the logic of his defense of science where he is perfectly aware he may be scandalizing his brother-scientists. His apologia for these scandalous proposals has, at first, a concise and allusive quality. There is no more reason for science to "blind itself" to these psychic properties than to "human freedom: one cannot even think of dispensing with human freedom unless one is a mechanist, and double-dyed" (VP 96/135). Behind those words one may infer Duhem's careful argument that "mechanism" was a metaphysical, not a scientific, view. Unless science decides to include these properties within its purview, Teilhard goes on to say, it will never succeed in explaining the evolutionary changes detected in the animal world, any more than a "purely determinist historian" can ever succeed in understanding the "historical adventures of human society" (VP

---

its very own—very much like Maxwell's notorious "demons"; life must be thought of as a "synthetic force superior in order" to the series of physico-chemical causes, all of which retain the efficacy of their own mode of activity. The scientist could, then, explain (analytically) all the workings of life in terms of those physico-chemical causes, much as one would explain the working of a watch purely in terms of the interaction of all its mechanical parts (compare Duhem's illustration in chap. 1, note 1, above). In both cases, however, there remains a further question, of a different "order" from the analytic question. Ask that higher-order question, and the answer called for is, in the one case, "a watch-maker," and, in the other, "life" considered as a *synthesizing* force. Monod, *Chance and Necessity*, pp. 25–33 and 59–61, discusses the same problem with little or no feel for such distinctions.

97/136). Purely "arguments from analogy," these two appeals to the sphere of the human? Not quite. For already forming in Teilhard's mind is the conviction that the "Science" of matter, mechanistic and determinist though it would claim to be, cannot remain forever divorced, in either focus or method, from the "sciences" of the human. The mechanistic "metaphysic" which physics wrongly espouses is precisely what prevents it from achieving its implicit goal of becoming a "total" scientific theory. The ground of that conviction we have already seen in glimmers: all scientific knowledge is "historical" knowledge, the knowledge, at various stages of its unfolding, of a single history, the history of cosmic matter evolving toward the consciousness and spontaneity which characterizes its human, or, better, "hominized," form. The laws of "growth" detectable through the observation of human societies, their stops and starts, their sideways leaps, their long periods of apparent stability before another leap takes place, are the same laws, fundamentally, as those which operate in the "mutations" of plant and animal populations. For if, as Teilhard is convinced his fellow-scientists also tacitly believe, observable reality is all made of the one "stuff," the case could not be otherwise.

This twin conviction of the unity of the observable real and the consequent *de jure* unity of "science" will eventually compel him to search for "laws" of evolutionary growth which can be "seen" as operative in the development of human societies, of plant and animal life, and even in the realm of atomic and subatomic matter: nothing less than that would be consistent with the fundamental insights to which he was driven in the course of defending the realism of scientific knowledge.

6

Entropy vs. Evolution

BY THE YEAR 1928, Teilhard's attention had been drawn
to the importance of an additional scientific anomaly. It
goes unmentioned in the "Hominization" essay of 1925,
making its earliest important appearance in the essay on
"The Movements of Life,"[1] written some three years after-
ward. It figures thereafter in both essays entitled "The Phenomenon of Man" (1928 and 1930 respectively),[2] and
then becomes a regular piece in the armory of Teilhard's
thinking.

The anomaly arises from the fact that physics proposes
a picture of the cosmos "running down" toward an eventual state of entropy, whereas the biologist in his study of
evolution is more regularly struck by the fact that life,
looked at "globally," represents a "current moving in the
opposite direction from entropy." The entropic drift Teilhard explains (VP 149/209; see also VP 167–69/233–34
and SC 94–95/125–26) as that "apparently inevitable
fall" whereby the corpuscular aggregates which physico-
chemistry studies appear to "slide," in accord with statistical laws of probability, toward a state in which all exchange
of useful energy fades out of the picture. Everything in our
observable world, physics would have us believe, is running
down toward this "death" of matter—everything, that is,
except life. Life, for its part, appears to work exactly opposite to entropy; instead of a play of chance factors bringing everything to the same flat level, life represents a me-

---

[1] Written in April 1928, and previously unpublished, this essay is printed
in VP (143–50/199–210).

[2] For the first essay bearing this title, see SC 86–97/115–28; for the second,
see VP 161–74/225–43.

thodical process of construction, erecting an edifice ever grander, increasingly defying the statistics of probability. The protozoa, metazoa, the stratum of social beings, humanity—these are all just so many gauntlets thrown down to flout entropy, all of them increasingly extravagant exceptions to the ways in which energetics and chance habitually operate.

Faced with the anomaly of these opposing movements, what account has science given them? Hitherto, Teilhard claims, science has striven to "close its eyes" or "turn them away" and to treat life as something forever to be excluded from the purview of physics. Life is merely an "abberration" refractory to mathematical explanation; hence, purely fortuitous and uninteresting for physics. And so the downward flow toward entropy remains, for the physicist, the only truly universal current, primordial and definitive, worth taking into account. Hence, life must be regarded as no more than a "bizarre disturbance," a purely accidental countercurrent within the larger current of entropic drift (VP 168/236).

Until now, that tactic may seem to have been successful; physics is content to see life as a merely "local" disturbance, and a kind of spindrift effect, a "weight which climbs upward but only on account of a heavier weight which is moving downward." Despite the "hitch" represented by this "local anomaly," physics persists in portraying nature's total system as flowing inexorably downward toward a "cold death" (VP 150/209).

But, suggests Teilhard, this tactic of reducing life to a mere local anomaly in the vast and all-embracing stream of entropy will not stand up against close scrutiny. If all we knew of life was the evidence gathered by a study, from "without," of the energy factors which probability theory includes in its equations, the anomaly might be less severe. But "there is another face of things to be considered": our own experience as living beings, coupled with the results of "scientific" investigations, concur in disclosing life as invariably mounting toward "ever-greater consciousness," a "within" factor which associates with, without being reducible to, the ever-increasing improbability the statisticians must admit to. A hasty look at the development of life might persuade one to think that "organic forms run hither and thither like so many countless waves," all more or less on the same level. But look beneath those wavemotions, and you see running a single, steady "tide," constantly rising toward "greater freedom, ingenuity, and thought."[3] Is it really thinkable that this "enormous happening" can be evaluated as no more than a "secondary effect" of the cosmic forces at work in our world? Can this tidal rise of life toward consciousness and freedom truly be relegated to the status of an "accessory feature of the universe"? "For metaphysics," Teilhard points out, "hesitation on this point is scarcely possible." But physics, for its part, "is only now coming to confront the question" (VP 150/210).

The two essays on "The Phenomenon of Man" return to this anomaly in slightly different terms: once looked on *as a whole*, the mounting spiral of life on earth, which reaches its paroxysm in humanity, is as "irreversible" as the irreversibility claimed for entropy itself (SC 94–95/125–26). Despite the stops and starts which the spiral goes through, it remains a "huge and undeniable fact" that the "ascent of part of the world toward states of increasing improbability" is too "regular" (VP 168–69/236–37) to be just some ephemeral countercurrent which the working of statistical laws will eventually put in its place—like a momentary tower of spindrift playing briefly in the sun but doomed, its moment passed, to subside and be absorbed into the downward wave from which it rose. His argument has taken a step forward: from the viewpoint of science as "natural history," the upward life-movement is too vast to

---

[3] On Duhem's use of this comparison, see above, chap. 5, note 9.

be merely "local," too "regular" for an aberration; it must be considered on an *equal footing*, at least, with the down-ward entropic drift. Hence, the scientific viewpoint which would make the entropic drift more "fundamental" than its competitor must be called into question. "If the universe confronts us with two important movements of elementary units," Teilhard hypothesizes,

> why not make the effort to see in this double current two phe-nomena of the same general scope, of the same importance, and of the same order: the two "faces" or two directions of the same extremely general happening? Why, when all is said, should life not be the "double," or the other side, of [the coin represented on one side by] entropy?[4]

He makes the suggestion in a hypothetical vein; but the very fact that the hypothesis, once entertained, has noth-ing absurd about it indicates that the regnant view holding entropy to be unquestionably the more general and im-portant of those two opposing movements—and therefore of a higher "order"—is far from unquestionable after all. We may be called upon to readjust that older view, and to see these opposing currents as of equal importance and generality: and, therefore, in terms of "classifying" them naturally, equal in "order."

But even in his manner of framing this suggestion, Teil-hard is already thinking of, or straining toward, a more de-veloped one.[5] There may, he will soon suggest, be just *one* vast process underway, with entropy and life development as the two "sides of the coin" as we look at it. The "classify-

---

[4] I suggest that the French term *face* was multivalent in Teilhard's use of it. Sometimes it can mean "countenance"; but on other occasions, as here, it conveys the notion of the "heads" side of a coin which necessarily entails a corresponding "tails" side—an "obverse," in our English expression, which im-plies a corresponding "reverse." One is reminded of the perfect mutuality of relation between form and matter in Aristotle's hylomorphic thought, an as-sociation which Teilhard expressly encouraged in VP 129*n*1/181*n*1.

[5] Despite the dualistic overtones of VP 170/238, Teilhard, as we shall see, comes to express this more unitary conception slightly farther on.

ing" power of that more unifying view is obviously inviting, and Teilhard will not take long in pursuing its lure.

And yet, the more conventional scientific view would urge, life as we know it on earth is so "local" and limited, so "fragile," and the universe of non-living matter so intimidatingly vast and solidly indestructible. How can these two unequals be placed on the same footing? Teilhard puts the question loyally, and endeavors to reply to it. One might have expected him to answer that to argue from the vastness of the non-living universe was to argue on the basis of purely quantitative considerations, and that "fragility" might just be the unavoidable concomitant of qualitative excellence. But however such replies might strike our sensibilities as the correct and inevitable ones, Teilhard's mind has made too large a voyage of thought to be entirely content with them.

He replies from the point of vantage he has won in the entire series of preceding essays. Taking humanity as the key to the evolutionary process which led up to the appearance of mankind, he points to the powers of thought, invention, and liberty as disclosing the "inner face" of the entire process. Had evolution never produced humanity, one might be entitled to ignore that inner face, and to explain its workings in terms of the "simple mechanisms" of conventional physics, rigidly determined in their operation and subject to all the hazards of chance. But seriously consider humanity as "continuous" with prehuman levels, both of life and of matter itself, and the undeniable appearance of thought discloses that there must have been some sort of consciousness, human liberty discloses there must have been some sort of spontaneity, and human inventiveness points to some measure of groping "ingenuity" at work in the prehuman phases of evolution. Life, once "hominized," unmasks itself as a "face, *sui generis*, of the World's potencies."

But this replies to the "localization" objection. For however local and confined terrene life (and humanity) may be in its overt "manifestations," the decisive point is that the "history" which went into its long preparation and eventual "success" is a history absolutely "co-extensive" with the history of cosmic matter in its entirety; for pre-living matter is where (and when!) it all began. The phenomenal web which science explores is an historical one, but also an unbroken one, such that no single phenomenon, however local, can be explained scientifically without bringing every single strand of the cosmic web into the account.

Yet life and humanity seem such "fragile" productions, and particularly so when viewed as "chance" products. What chance has created it may just as swiftly destroy. But this, once again, is to view life purely from the "outside." Focus once on the "inner" face of the entire process, and you catch sight of consciousness, spontaneity, and ingenuity discreetly at work, with a strategy whose "sureness" and "patient infallibility" conducted the upward march of living forms to the human level. "Something as irresistible as Matter itself," Teilhard asks us to see, a "current" as powerful as the current of entropy, was for all those billion years in secret control of the process (VP 169/237).[6]

This way of relating entropy and evolution as two co-ordinate cosmic currents resembles, Teilhard observes, a rejuvenated form of those "dualisms" common in ancient thought-ways, somewhat as the modern atomic theory renewed by transforming the cruder ancient atomisms of Democritus and Lucretius (VP 170/238). Instead of condemning, that ancient heritage may actually commend this dualistic solution. So at least he seems to be suggesting; and still his mind continues to work toward a more unifying

[6] Teilhard speaks here of the somewhat "childish" tendency to situate the most solid and enduring realities of our cosmos on the levels of the "most probable" molecular combinations. One cannot but think of his own childhood attachment to his God of iron and rock; see again the title essay in HM for this episode and for its significance in his own development.

and unitary way of relating them. The evolutionary current may run "through," or "alongside," the entropic; or it may be that both of them are "reducible" to some "third, more general movement," still to be identified (SC 95/126). In any event, looking at them both through the "breach" or "rent" in cosmic matter provided by the human phenomenon, we are able, with new eyes, to see the anti-entropic stream as "at least one of the two primary *élans* which draw the world along" (SC 95n1/126n1).

But even in 1928, Teilhard is tempted to go farther than that. It may be, he writes in a footnote, that this "imponderable current of spirit," only "masked" in its operations among lower material realities, is even more "fundamental" than the entropic current; that a play of "liberty," "spontaneity"—something akin to the "indeterminism" of a later physics—is operative beneath the "determinisms" and "mechanisms" which sciences of matter, by reason of their method, imagine as uniquely operative (see SC 95n1/126n1).[7] Follow up on this proposal (as Teilhard himself does, in time), and the earliest phase of evolutionary history takes the form of a cosmic drama already underway; matter now consists of a "myriad of elementary spontaneities" caught up in a "play of large numbers." Look at such a crowd movement from a great height, and study it quantitatively as contemporary physics did in Teilhard's time, and the crowd will seem to move in ways which are mathematically determined. Indeed, if the individual spontaneities are only of an "elementary" and minimally developed kind, each of them will be additionally restricted in its scope of action and "carried along," as it were, by those crowd movements. For "individuality" at this lowest level is so feebly developed that the bonding of each element into the crowd as a whole can in actual fact dominate the element's individual activity, without, however, completely stamping out all spark of spontaneity.

[7] See also chap. 7, note 12, below.

Endow each of these "spontaneities" with an equally minimal quantum of consciousness, ingenuity, and conspirational power, as the presence of those properties in the human phenomenon suggests, and the lines of this cosmic drama take hesitant shape: each element is thrusting, groping, along with all its fellows, for some opening toward a higher mode of being and life, meaning a more developed consciousness and liberty of action. The "successes" at this level are understandably very, very few; yet physics and chemistry assure us that a tiny minority of these elements succeeded in achieving that superior mode of bonding found among mega-molecules, polymers, and later among cells, protozoa—and, eventually, human beings. "Seeing" this way, from "within," we are entitled to view the upward spiral as the *primary* movement of cosmic matter; entropic drift now takes definitely second billing. It represents the vast, inevitably vast, amount of "wastage" one should expect to find issuing from this earliest and least "ingenious" phase of natural history.

That, briefly put, is the solution to the evolution–entropy anomaly which Teilhard will eventually put forward in *The Phenomenon of Man*. But the pieces were all in place as early as the year 1928.

7

Toward a New Science
of the Past

IN THE COURSE OF HIS ANSWER to Vialleton's claim that
evolution might be just an "illusion," Teilhard makes a
series of admissions which at first appear somewhat puz-
zling. "Illusion," he asks Vialleton, "that one zoological
species flows into another?" and answers, *Passe*. "Illusion,"
he goes on, "the general ascent" of form after form "and
always toward greater consciousness and spontaneity?"
Passe encore, he replies, and comments that this view of
the matter is "too impregnated with philosophy, even a
sort of mysticism, to prevent a purely scientific mind from
perceiving in the modifications which life has undergone
no more than the workings of simple diversification." The
impression which the hurried reader[1] might glean from this
passage is that Teilhard is convinced of neither of these
two propositions, and is willing to discard them both. But
situate them in the context of his argument, and the French
term *passe* clearly functions otherwise: he does not mean
to "concede" that these two views of the evolutionary process represent "illusions," but only that it would not be
appropriate to defend them here and now. Only after he
has shown Vialleton that living beings constitute an "ordered, organized distribution" both temporally and spa-
tially, that evolution actually happened, does he reserve
the right to return to an examination of these two ways of
understanding "how" evolution may have taken place.

[1] The same impression might result from Cohen's loose "I grant it" in VP
86–87; compare the French version, p. 123.

Establishing that "order and organization" prevail among its products, then, is a first and necessary step toward proving *that* evolution occurred. But *how* could it have occurred in such a way as to leave the fossil evidence in the shape it *de facto* assumed? To Vialleton's protestation of impossibility, we saw that Teilhard replies with his reflections on mutation theory: to a counterclaim of impossibility, it was legitimate to reply that the thing could be shown both possible and plausible. So far, so good. But the kind of mutations to which Teilhard was compelled to resort were themselves suspect, in their workings and implications, to the "purely scientific mind," even, perhaps, as suspect as the second of the pair of views he has abstained from arguing with Vialleton. Yet far from being hostile toward viewing evolution as an ascent toward greater complexity and consciousness, Teilhard will show, in an unpublished essay written a year later,[2] considerable sympathy toward it. Indeed, it is the view presiding over *The Phenomenon of Man*. How did Teilhard, in the meantime, come to hope that scientists might accept it? The essay entitled "Hominization" may answer part of that question; it is, at all events, the most important single building block for understanding the method he was eventually to apply in *The Phenomenon of Man*.

He opens this essay, which remained unpublished until its appearance among his collected works, by disclaiming any metaphysical or philosophical preoccupations; he will conduct his argument on the "phenomenal" level proper to science. But, he points out, there is a profoundly anomalous rift in the fabric of science itself; indeed it is highly questionable whether one can speak of "science" in the singular at all! For despite the intimate linkage which all

---

[2] The date attribution (1923) in VP is erroneous. See Claude Cuénot, *Teilhard de Chardin: A Biographical Study*, trans. Vincent Colimore, ed. René Hague (Baltimore: Helicon, 1965), pp. 422–23, correcting the date he gave in the French original of that work (*Pierre Teilhard de Chardin: Les Grandes Etapes de son évolution* [Paris: Plon, 1958]).

scientists *qua* scientists must admit between humanity and the infrahuman levels of nature from which humanity evolved, there is no corresponding linkage among the sciences of nature and the sciences of humanity. On the one hand, physics, chemistry, and for the most part biology explore the properties—and therefore the evolutionary "history"—of the infrahuman levels of cosmic matter; anatomy, physiology, psychology, and sociology, on the other, direct their explorations at humanity. But in this division of labor both sets of sciences treat humanity as though it constituted an entirely different world from the world of infrahuman nature, and one to be regarded from an entirely different "point of view" from the viewpoint prevalent among the sciences of nature. How can scientists reconcile themselves to the inconsistency implied by exploring two levels of phenomena in our unitary evolving universe in two such markedly different manners?

Now, it is quite conceivable that Teilhard was writing this essay, as he often did, to clarify and give initial formulation to his own ideas. We are more than ever entitled to suppose, then, that he is writing it out of his convictions concerning the unbroken unity of the phenomenal real, the "historical" nature both of that evolving real and of the sciences which explore it on the varied strata of its development, and the ideal unity of science itself as a "Natural History," engaged in the task of finding "natural classifications" based on the "physical" connections between those various sectors of phenomenal reality. Once all these related convictions are taken into account, the anomaly, if not the scandal, of writing that "natural history" in two separate languages, so to speak, becomes a real one. Science has no right to keep double accounts, one for its human family-members, the other for the nature which, far from being some alien domain, is the womb which gave humanity birth.

But, he must admit, there are two sciences at least which initially seem to escape his indictment, for both anatomy and morphology at least attempt to respect man's linkage, and compare his features, with infrahuman life-forms. But to what end? To find, obviously, a "natural classification" which does justice to man's unity with and differences from those other products of evolutionary development. But how well have they succeeded in that task? Only very inadequately, Teilhard contends; their classification of the human group is, strictly on scientific grounds, demonstrably unsatisfactory. This, he claims, can be shown by applying the canons of the strict "naturalist" or scientific "systematician." Teilhard here speaks of according the human group its proper "value"; but the value he refers to has nothing to do with the "value" which philosophy, religion, or any "spiritual thesis" would insist on according human dignity. The term is drawn from systematics, where a "genus" classification implies a value "higher" than that of the more limited "species" subclasses grouped "under" it. His aim is to argue for "increasing" the value of humanity as a group of life forms in the classificatory scheme of natural history; his unique business here is that of "saving science" (VP 62/ 91).[3] But to save science overall, he must show how the rift among the sciences can be healed; this in turn means that he must eventually propose a uniform "point of view" and single-account "manner" for science's study of the entire skein of the phenomenal real. A large order, so he will start small; if he can make it plain what "natural classification" the human group truly merits in the science of systematics, it may lead him to uncover the deficiencies in the approaches which anatomy and morphology have taken, precisely those deficiencies which led them to mis-classify humanity. Correct those deficiencies, and we may be a

[3] Comparison will show that up to this point I have been merely summarizing the content of this essay.

giant step closer to recognizing the corrections to apply in "scientific method" overall, and may heal the rift in science itself.

The first step in this process is to clear our minds, and genuinely adopt, for once, the attitude of the "pure naturalist" (or natural historian), and out of that attitude, to take the same completely fresh look at the earthly human group as some alien intelligence just arrived from outer space would. We must try to look at ourselves as though seeing for the first time some unfamiliar species heretofore undiscovered. A difficult adjustment of our vision,[4] Teilhard admits; but add nothing to what you see, and leave out nothing of what you see. What, now, do you see? From a purely "experimental"[5] point of view, Teilhard suggests, we see some surprising things.

First, we behold a group of life forms differing in bodily features astonishingly little from the other animal forms from which it emerged—far, far less, for instance, than birds differ from their reptile forebears. How then, bearing in mind only these somatic properties, would one "classify" humanity? Why, very much as present-day naturalists do: as no more than a "family" or "sub-order" of the larger group of "primates."

Now, however, look once again. But this time look with eyes educated to "natural history" as, precisely, *history*. This single human group, so simple and homogeneous when compared with the heterogeneous collection of amphibians and reptiles which accomplished a similar feat in vanished ages, represents a "vital success" otherwise unparalleled in evolutionary history: in an amazingly short

[4] He makes an interesting comparison here (VP 52/78); the readjustment he asks for is somewhat like the one required of a physicist or biologist, accustomed to dealing with the "infinitely small," when asked to reconcile what he sees under his microscope with the world of beings seen life-size. Compare the gap between the analytic and the synthetic–holist ways of "seeing"; it may not, after all, be quite that easy for a molecular biologist like Monod or Medawar to succeed in seeing what Teilhard is asking him to see!

[5] Recall once again the ambiguity of this term, discussed above, pp. 48–49.

period of geological time, it has "invaded" and conquered every corner of our globe, either eliminating or assimilating every other form of competing animal life. In short, never, in any preceding geological epoch, did any single instance of higher living forms succeed in "occupying the earth so extensively as Man." Now, this historical conquest is a "brutal, tangible fact," so tangible and undeniably factual as to satisfy the most positivist of positivists (VP 56/83).

Thus far, however, we have focused on the more quantitative aspects of the human invasion: on the time, and geographical extension which it took. Now focus on the "qualitative" side of the matter, but staying—as a good natural historian must—with "strictly experimental" qualities, qualities which lend themselves indisputably to scientific observation.[6]

The first such qualitative property is the use, by the human group, of "tools"—but in an entirely revolutionary way when compared with the infrahuman orders of life. For animals rather "become" tools, specialize in such a way as to become burrowers, flyers, swimmers, what have you; the entire animal takes the somatic form adapted to its specialized kind of activity. The human group, without itself becoming somatically specialized, and therefore limited to this or that form of activity, devised instruments which remained "exterior" to their users: whence a versatility and intensification of potency which surely accounts in great part for the swift and all-conquering "invasion" the history of this group represents.

But along with that evolutionary "success," the invention of tools resulted, apparently, in a sudden decrease in

---

[6] This recognition of the "qualitative" as accessible to, and indispensable for, any comprehensive scientific synthesis, was a point which Duhem had also stressed (see his *Aim and Structure*, trans. Wiener, pp. 110–13, 307–308). That contention relates closely to the wider notion of "experiment" (see note 5 above) and the rejection of mechanism as a "metaphysical" rather than a truly scientific view, common to Teilhard and Duhem. See chap. 1, notes 5 and 6, above.

the power which living organisms formerly possessed to "evolve" into physically novel forms. We noted, at the outset, that humans differ, physically, very little from their closest primate ancestors; now the reason for the slightness of that morphological transformation is clear: it was not needed. To attain the "vital success" which it has achieved, the human group did not need to evolve physically (literally) to *become* the variety of interrelated and interdependent specialists—burrowers, climbers, flyers, and all the rest—into which every previously successful "branch" of the tree of life found it necessary to "diverge" and "radiate." Every human being has the power now to "be" a climber, underwater swimmer, or flyer, without undergoing the physical transformation which would enslave him to this or that unique and limited specialization (VP 56–58/84–86).

But, one might object, we are talking now about the "artificial" as opposed to the "natural." The airplane which permits a human being to fly is as "artificial" as the submarine which enables him to become an underwater swimmer. It will not do to claim that humanity has diversified into swimmers, flyers, burrowers, and the rest, "naturally" —the way, for instance, the Australian marsupials seem to have done, and thereby assured their own evolutionary "success."

Is that distinction, though, Teilhard replies, so absolute, so hard and fast, as our possibly outworn ways of thinking would make it? Is there no "deeper linkage" *whatever* between the evolutionary transformation of reptile into flyer, and the human group's invention of the airplane? Could it not be that this little thought-experiment we are embarking on may require a fresh and revolutionary readjustment of ideas, a readjustment which compels our asking whether it is "natural" for the human group to diversify and radiate "artificially"? Could it not be that for humankind the artificial has *become* the natural?

Indeed, this "naturalization" of the artificial may precisely be one of the signs that in producing the human group evolution has reached a dramatically new phase. Furthermore, it points the way to resolving the anomaly we began with. For there is a staggering disproportion between the slight morphological shifts which encourage the naturalist to rank humanity as a mere "family" or "suborder" of the primates, and the greatness of humanity's evolutionary success: this historical "invasion" which so swiftly made humanity a veritable sheet or wave of life sweeping across the face of our globe, mastering every competing form of life, and with mines and farms, irrigation systems and erosion controls, bridges and telegraph, airplanes and radio, laboratories and factories, transmuting the form, and very materials, of our planet. Once entertain the possibility that evolutionary history has, with the arrival of humanity, entered on a new phase entirely, and the invitation to shatter habitual distinctions and bygone categories has nothing scandalous about it. Then, admit that evolution's advance has produced a group for whom "artificial" diversification is as natural *to it* as morphological diversification was to infrahuman forms, and it becomes possible to conceive of a fresh "natural classification" of evolutionary life-forms to which the astonishing success of the human group entitles it. It becomes both possible and necessary, in fact, to envisage a new "systematics" which would rank humanity as nothing less than a new zoological "order." Nothing less than that rank will fit the facts; but perhaps the facts warrant something even more.[7]

Now Teilhard takes a step which calls on our powers to envisage humanity as a "Whole": a single, interdependent, "organic" unit of life. He recalls how science is compelled to do this sort of thinking on other levels of evolutionary reality, and most notably with respect to the life of animal

[7] We shall see as his argument continues that he comes to realize that an even more radical adjustment is needed.

"species" as such. The example of the entire "branch" of Australian marsupials is one case in point; but it is nearly impossible to observe the behavior of social insects, like the ants, without being compelled to entertain the notion of some "collective forces" mysteriously coordinating the behavior of the group precisely as a group.

Shall we compare humanity to an anthill, therefore? Yes, affirms Teilhard; *but*, or, rather, two such "buts," and both of them of decisive importance. First, no anthill has achieved the universal extension which humanity enjoys; and, secondly, humanity, unlike the anthill, is furnished with special "organs" of linkage which not only facilitate rapid communication from individual to individual, or sub-group to subgroup, but act in such a way as little by little to transform the totality of the human group, gradually turning it from a mere aggregate of individuals and sub-groups into a kind of single "organism."

Only a metaphor? Not quite, claims Teilhard. But again, we must remember to rejuvenate our vision of what is going on by jettisoning the hard and fast "natural vs. artificial" distinction. Think of the so-called "artificial" as the "humanized natural," and the airplane becomes the genuine *analogue* of the bird; the submarine, the analogue of the fish; and so on down the list of human inventions. But by the same token, we are jolted suddenly into seeing roads, air- and sea-lanes, radios and telegraph lines as constituting a "veritable nervous system for Humanity" as a single living organism, the substrate of a "common consciousness of the human multitude" looked on as a whole. Seen this way, the network of linkages bringing humanity ever closer together bears startling resemblance to the way biological evolution has managed to ensure the unity of every physical organism it ever constructed in the past; we are, in short, watching biological evolution continue its work in present human history.

Seen in this new light, libraries become the repository of humanity's corporate "memory"; education, the process of elaborating humanity's corporate "heredity"; and so forth. Again, not merely metaphors, but genuine analogies. It would be easy to exaggerate such analogies, granted; but it would be just as unwarranted to underestimate them, and dangerous to deny them all force whatever. But what is the root from which all these constructions spring? A twin root, Teilhard suggests, "two special psychic factors": "reflection" and (in Edouard Le Roy's coinage) "conspiration." And both these factors, he claims, are as evident to scientific observation as any sort of measurable energy you can name (VP 60–61/88–89).

For consider the observable fact that humans have invented tools and thereby ensured their successful occupation of our globe. Isn't it obvious that such invention springs from "the power every human consciousness has to reflect upon itself in order to recognize the conditions and workings of its own activity" (VP 60/88)? Consider, furthermore, the equally observable, but entirely novel, kind of "linkages" which set the human group apart from all other living groups on earth; where else do these originate but from the power which diverse human centers of consciousness possess to "join up" with each other— through language communication, for instance, and through a million other ways of bonding—so that every single individual becomes reflectively aware of his or her unity with all other members of the human group, and with the human group considered as a "single whole"?

Now, it is crucial for evaluating the case which Teilhard is making in this pivotal essay, and the method which he eventually employs in *The Phenomenon of Man*, to notice that he proposes that these two "properties" of the human group—reflection and conspiration as he has defined and illustrated them—are accessible to the kind of observation which science already habitually employs.[8] He has not once, he claims, taken leave of the terrain of what science considers as "factual." But establishing the factual reality of these two properties, psychic properties though they be, is as far (he affirms) as scientific observation can carry us.

Grant him that much, for the sake of argument at least. Where does the next step of his argument lead? We have seen him argue that the morphological diversity of the human group (if one accepts "artificial" diversification as the humanized version of the "natural") warrants ranking it a new zoological "order," at least. Now, he must turn to ask whether even that ranking suffices to reduce the anomaly which "systematics" has on its hands. He resumes the evidence and argumentative steps which led to ranking humanity as a zoological "order" *at least*; but now he concludes that even that promotion in systematic rank does not go so far as the evidence warrants. Carnivores and rodents constitute just such an "order" inside the larger "class" of mammals, but humanity's diversity runs as wide as that of the entire class of mammals. Will it suffice, then, to admit that systematics should rank humanity as a "class"?

Not quite, Teilhard avers. For while introducing a bothersome disharmony into the reigning scheme of zoological classification, this strategy would have a second disadvantage as well: it would still fail to do justice to the systematic value and specific novelty represented by the human group. The systematic disharmony amounts to this: accord humanity the value of an order or class, and you are simply following the rules of a systematics which both assumes and implies that any change in activity specialization always and everywhere correlates with a change in organic, morphological, specialization. But while the rules of that kind of systematics may hold for the infrahuman levels of

[8] Teilhard would point here to the "sciences" of humanity such as history, sociology, or psychology; geology–paleontology would occupy a similar position. See above, pp. 83, 94.

evolutionary development—for the excellent reason that systematics was originally devised with the aim of "naturally classifying" the items of that infrahuman level and only those items—this is the very correlation which, the evidence shows, is no longer operative when we take seriously the "artificial–natural" mode of diversification proper and peculiar to the human group! The jaggedness of that systematic "fit," moreover, comes precisely from ignoring the "specific novelty" which humanity represents when compared with all and every infrahuman class and order of life forms: the psychic properties of reflection and conspiration which account for humanity's "importance" in the light of facts which experimental biology cannot deny or wish away.

Now at last we have taken the full measure of the anomaly which humanity constitutes for the systematician, and for science more generally. Is there any way of dissolving this anomaly, any way of "saving science"?

If science is to be saved, Teilhard now proposes, two conditions must be met. On the one hand, we must somehow continue to do justice to the classifying "value" which the older systematics accorded to somatic characteristics in its effort to "hierarchize" the array of living forms; but we must simultaneously, on the other hand, do justice to the "supreme originality," the "specific novelty," of this phenomenon, the human group—and do so while respecting its profound "rootedness" in the world of our experience (VP 62/91). The second of those requirements flows directly from the evidence and argument Teilhard has so far adduced, and from the obvious rule in any good classificatory system demanding that a species be set off from the other members of its wider class (its genus, for example) by probing for, and accurately locating, its *real* "specific difference." The language is as old as Aristotle, but the import as modern as Duhem's theory of "natural," rather than arbitrary and artificial, classification. And the underlying issue is what it has been for Teilhard from the outset, to "save science" in the only way he thinks it can be saved: by keeping it faithful to the demands of "natural classification." For only on that condition, he is persuaded, can one make any grounded claim that science tells us something about the way things really are.

So much for the second. But why does Teilhard insist on the first requirement, that of salvaging so much of the older "systematics"? Again, he remains consistent with his earlier conviction: that no outworn scientific theory is ever completely outworn. The historic procession of scientific models always requires that the succeeding model be careful to preserve everything of reality value in the model it replaces. Merely a streak of timidity showing up in this radical proposal for mounting a scientific revolution? Not a bit of it. Teilhard is acutely aware of the tight-rope walk involved in continuing to defend scientific "realism." Specifically, he is convinced, as any naturalist must be, that systematics and natural history were not completely wrong; the study of somatic variations *did* succeed in establishing an impressive "natural classification" of the array of infrahuman life-forms. Just as Leverrier's Neptune became an "imposed factor" which every later and more advanced astronomical system had to assimilate, so here the older systematics can be transcended properly only if its undeniable achievements undergo a similar assimilation by whatever "new" systematics takes its place.

But any new and more adequate systematics must also respect the profound "rootedness" of humanity as a "phenomenon" in the world of our phenomenal experience. That giveaway clause alerts us to another "audience" which this essay[9] had to keep in mind. The conviction behind the phrase is familiar: the phenomenal real which the scientist

---

[9] Even an essay written for oneself can have some limited and special imaginary "audience" in view, of course.

qua scientist is committed to exploring is a single unbroken web stretching always farther back into space–time, supposing no "first" member in the sequence, nor admitting of any subsequent member whose appearance in the network can be accounted for (scientifically) except by an appeal to the total historical sequence of all preceding members. This, Teilhard is confident, is the tacit postulate which he shares with his fellow natural scientists who catalogue humanity among the various other groups of living beings by inspecting purely "somatic characteristics." But he is not free to ignore the tenants of a more "spiritual" view of man who constantly insist on those aspects—call them reflection and conspiration or consciousness and freedom—which constitute, in their eyes, humanity's "supreme originality." That one-sided stress prompts them, accordingly, to ignore entirely or even to oppose the findings of their opposite numbers, humanity's "profound rootedness in the world" of scientific experience, and, consequently, the evolutionary explanation of humanity's origins.

The dichotomy implied here goes back to one of the earliest writings we have from Teilhard's pen, the article on "man" which he was asked to write for the *Dictionnaire apologétique de la foi catholique* in 1909.[10] There he sets forth the view of man adopted by those (scientists, one presumes) who view the human purely from "without," and contrasts it with the counterview proposed, presumably, by philosophers and theologians; looking at human reality from "within," and accenting the "spiritual" qualities of the human, they often enough conclude that an evolutionary view is irreducibly inimical to according those spiritual

[10] D'Ouince, *Un Prophète en procès*, I 57n17, correctly stresses the high regard his masters must have had for Teilhard's competence in theology to recommend him to Father A. D'Alès (the editor of the *Dictionnaire apologétique*) as capable of authoring this important article—and to recommend him in preference to those future theological luminaries with whom he was then studying.

qualities the value and importance entitled to them. So they feel warranted in ignoring, or even opposing, the evolutionary view.

It should be noted that Teilhard could easily have rested content with tracing these divergent views to the diversity of disciplines and their differing points of view, foci of interest, and resulting canons of both evidence and method. If science chooses, as it quite properly might, to confine itself to studying those aspects of reality which are publicly observable by controlled experiments whose results in turn must be expressible in quantitative measurements, then it must at the same time recognize lucidly what that choice implies: an incomplete survey of the evidence and a seriously constricting manner of handling even that incomplete survey. It might just be that equally, or more, significant evidence is the "private" kind which every human finds to hand when looking "inside" to the workings of reflection, intention, and choice; that what is uncovered by such introspective observation is amenable neither to public verification by others nor to mathematical measurement and correlation. Let philosophers and theologians, then, study man in a way which complements the scientific, and erect their quite contrasting vision of man accordingly. Teilhard could have contented himself with pointing out that such views do not genuinely contradict, but merely complement, the scientific view of humanity—and vice versa.

Had he contented himself with this solution to the question, Teilhard might today have far more friends among scientists, philosophers, and theologians. Doubtless, but he would not have been Teilhard. He alludes constantly to the differences in the scientific, philosophical, and theological disciplines; he insists that they must be kept distinct —their pictures of the world must never be "confused," and one cannot rightly ask any one of them to perform the task which is proper to another. And yet, though they must never be "confused" one with another, science and philosophy do, and must, "converge." Teilhard could not remain satisfied with two images of humanity which ran so counter to each other as to give the clear, even if only *prima facie*, impression that they stood in blatant contradiction to each other.

That instinct of his, it may be fairly argued, does him signal credit; but far from being a purely "scientific" attitude, it owes far more than appears on the surface to a genuinely philosophic concern: that of safeguarding the "realism" of scientific knowledge. Teilhard will eventually appeal to philosophers to take more seriously the evolutionary view of "phenomena" presented by science; now he sets about convincing the scientists that they, too, have some readjusting to do, that they must take some account of what the philosophers discover when they view man from "within." The question is, can he present precisely *scientific* warrant for making this latter suggestion to his fellow-scientists? The first step he takes in that direction is aimed at resolving the anomaly which he has endeavored to outline when it comes precisely to finding a "natural classification" for the human group. The older classificatory schemas won't do, except for the infrahuman orders of life; so, preserving their application for the infrahuman, Teilhard proposes thinking in terms of a radically new set of categories, categories "*hors pair*," which can encompass the older system of classification without distorting it or doing violence to the facts it seeks to respect: the facts arguing for humanity's unbreakable links to the "general development of life." Those new categories, though, must do equal justice to the "absolutely new phase" in that life development which, we have now been persuaded to acknowledge, humanity constitutes.

Try thinking, Teilhard suggests, of the natural history of our entire planet as passing through three vast phases, each phase leaving that planet vested with a kind of "en-

velope": a "zone," "circle," or "sphere." The first of those
"spheres" we may term the "lithosphere," the rocky crust
which Suess described as resulting from the incredibly long
process whereby continents formed. But now consider that
process of "continentalization" as the necessary preliminary to a second: the emergence, proliferation, and spread
over the lithosphere of a second envelope, the envelope of
"life" in all its varied forms, from grass to chimpanzee—
what Suess was brought to term the "biosphere." Now take
one final step, one which Suess stopped short of taking, and
yet required of us by the classificatory anomaly which the
facts of the human "invasion" of our planet compel us to
deal with. Consider that human invasion and total occupation of our planet as covering that planet with a third,
"psychic," envelope, an envelope characterized by those
startlingly novel properties of reflection and conspiration;
call this third planetary envelope the "Noosphere."

Now examine what this new classificatory schema manages to achieve. All that is true in our former classification
of infrahuman life-forms fits easily into the "biospheric"
envelope; but that envelope in turn has now been situated
in its relationship to the evolution of infra-living matter
which went before it. The "sphere" category permits of expressing the linkage of organic life to the womb of pre-
organic matter from which, "natural history" assures us,
it emerged. Instead of hanging in mid-air, as it were, the
"world" which biology explores has been rooted in the pre-
biological world of physics, chemistry, and biochemistry;
these sciences have automatically become connected chapters in natural "history."

Before turning to examine how this schema manages to
classify humanity, however, consider for a moment that
process whereby "biospheric" realities emerged from the
lithospheric level. Surely that emergence must be counted
as a revolutionary change of state which affected the pre-
living cosmic matter which preceded and went into living

beings. That same matter went into the change; we are compelled to acknowledge an element of "continuity" in the process. And yet the change of state was a truly revolutionary one; it tempts us at first to think of living matter as almost utterly discontinuous with what went before. Continuity in discontinuity: how are we to conceptualize such a seeming paradox?

Philosophers have wrestled with such paradoxes since Thales announced that matter and especially organic matter acted like something "filled with gods"; but scientists too are familiar with similar paradoxes. Consider a geometric figure, like a conic surface. Start at the base and cut a section through the cone; that section will have a certain circumference expressible by a number. Now cut a section higher on the cone; the circumference is reduced, but still it has some measurable value. But run your section-cuts upward along the axis of the cone, and all at once you are faced no longer with a circumference but with a point, a point to which no quantitative value can be applied. You have, by a continuous process, been vaulted into a new order of realities: continuity generating a leap into apparent discontinuity. And yet, discontinuity of this sort does not imply a "rupture"; the apex of the cone is the point at which a "change of state" asserts itself, somewhat as water, continuously heated, changes state and escapes as steam. Think of it as a "threshold" whose very function as threshold is to divide, and at the same time to unite one room with another; we approach a threshold in that continuous movement called walking, so that "on" the threshold itself we find ourselves passing from one room to another. Again, there is discontinuity in continuity, with no "rupture" in the continuous movement of walking.

The transformation of pre-living into living matter, then, represents a first "critical threshold" traversed by evolutionary history in its advance. Some might say that the passage from non-conscious to "conscious" life represented a second such threshold. However that may be, the evolutionary emergence and spread of reflective and conspiring humanity on our planet unquestionably represent a change as revolutionary as the passage from pre-life to life: another "critical threshold" in natural history, the threshold which was crossed when the "noospheric" envelope began its brush-fire sweep over the surface of the biosphere. Linked to the lithosphere and biosphere, and without any severance of that linkage, humanity manifests at once the very "ancient" characteristics evolutionists point to as inherited from those spheres, as well as the "absolutely novel" characteristics which persuade some "spiritualist" thinkers to conceive of humanity as a piece of flotsam on the surface of time's vast ocean, with no roots reaching downward into what went on before. This concept of "critical threshold," then, coupled with the tri-phase development of planetary "spheres," not only provides a "natural classification" for all the products of evolution's history, it also goes a long way to resolving that other anomaly: the disrelation between the "science" of matter and the "sciences" of man. And now, there is yet another anomaly: the opposition between evolutionary scientists and spiritualist philosophers.

But the scientific task of elaborating these two classificatory notions—"spheres" and "critical thresholds"—in order to accommodate the scientific facts has compelled us to think of humanity's emergence as the result of a labor of generation on the part of Earth itself and Life as a "whole." That emergence corresponds to the liberation of a new terrestrial potency; every infrahuman life-activity achieves freshened and super-animated form with the emergence of the human. This implies, however, that we must now view humanity as a phase or stage toward which both terrestrial matter and terrestrial life were "constrained" to proceed in order to attain the "balance" required, not for the vital success of this or that species, but for the vital success of the entire evolutionary process. Reducing the double anomaly facing us at the outset of this essay has involved our thinking of humanity, life, terrestrial matter, evolution, and natural history as "wholes"—and, one might add, thinking of them that way with a vengeance!

The first of those anomalies was the inability which conventional systematics manifested to find a satisfactory way of classifying humanity: there was a manifest disproportion between the biological "importance" of the human group in the history of our planet and the "value" which systematics accorded humanity as a mere "family" or subgroup of the primates. This anomaly Teilhard feels he has traced to three connected methodological defects: the omission, first of all, of reflection and conspiration, of all but somatic factors, as classificatory phenomena; the failure, secondly, to deal with the "artificial" as the form which the "natural" must take on the human level; and, thirdly, the resulting failure to apply the fresh conceptual tools required by a problem which compels us to think in terms of "spheres" and "critical thresholds" in order to take adequate account of both the biosphere's linkage with, yet radical distinction from, the lithosphere, and, coordinately, the noosphere's rootedness in, yet startling novelty when compared with, everything on the biospheric level.

Application of these conceptual tools, he further suggests, may go a considerable way toward eliminating the anomaly represented by the disunity reigning among the various sciences. Accept the adjustments already suggested, and capitalize on humanity's profound continuity with preceding products of the evolutionary process, and then it becomes thinkable to take humanity as the "key" to Evolution's ways of working at all levels of reality. The proposal should not seem all that strange; the evolutionary scientist is already familiar with taking the vertebrates as just such a privileged focus for illuminating the fact that evolution happened on the animal level. Furthermore, that same proposal only underlines the oddity of our more conventional assumption that we shall glean more certain knowledge of the real by focusing on what is most "tangible" in our universe, pre-living matter. How utterly strange that world really is to us; when we reflect upon it, how distant and alien—and for that very reason, how impoverished a yield of information it presents us with about the working of life and evolution in its more significant phases. Humanity, however, is what is closest and most familiar to us, in time and evolutionary "age." As the vertebrates for just such reasons of closeness render more eloquent testimony to evolution on the biospheric levels, so, *a fortiori*, this latest chapter in evolutionary history, humanity, represents an ensemble of evidence which is still intact, and an evolutionary product still in the process of active formation. In addition, the nature of human activity is most "knowable" for us in that, alone among the various levels of the evolutionary real, we know its workings from "within." Doesn't the bold exploitation of that interior acquaintance offer the richest promise for uncovering the inmost "springs" of evolution's ways of working?

Teilhard goes on to illustrate his claim by reading what we know of human history in "zoological" terms. We find the same sorts of harmonies along with paradoxes to which Vialleton had pointed in the fossil record: "waves" of life interfering with and relaying each other, births of nations and cultures, vanishing peduncles, branchings and expansions of human waves which end, so often, in the kinds of dissociation and scleroses also found in the fossil record. But the evidence for these incontestably evolutionary movements we find *more clearly* in human history than anywhere in the record of any group which preceded it in time! Why not, then, take advantage of these analogies—not merely, mind you, literary metaphors (VP 62/90–91)[11]—

---

[11] Teilhard makes a distinction here (VP 63/92) whose importance seems to have grown on him: scientific resistance to literary metaphors must not be allowed to exclude appeal to genuine analogies. Discriminating between

frankly focus on humanity, and pursue the inquiry about how evolution operates on every level by concentrated study of its operations in the group most known to us?

Accept this reversal of the usual scientific method, however, and evolution immediately changes its aspect on every level. It now takes on the appearance of the dominantly "psychic" phenomenon it clearly is on the human level; morphological changes on lower levels now suggest themselves as exterior results of psychic thrust, invention, and development; and the rigid "determinisms" science hitherto thought to "find" on lower levels of reality now show up as a myriad of "spontaneities" in swarming quest of increased consciousness, greater spontaneity, and, ultimately, the "liberty" manifest in humanity.[12]

The view resulting from this total readjustment of focus and perspective has a further result. It goes a long way to resolving a third anomaly which no reflective scientist can entirely ignore: the nagging opposition between the scientist's insistence on humanity's continuity with its animal forebears, and the spiritualistic thinker's equally deter-

---

the two, it must be admitted, requires a nice sense of judgment, somewhat like the judgment involved in discriminating between promising and unpromising hypotheses in order to select the ones worth putting to experimental test. (Again, comparison with the text will show that the preceding pages are only a running summary of the argument of "Hominization.")

[12] What Teilhard is calling for here is a change in the "form" of thinking which we bring to the evidence being surveyed; that basic insight goes back to his earliest essay, which traced the apparent "exactitude" of physical laws to the mathematical form of thought which physics applied to its experimental results. Now he is reminding the reader that the same thing holds for the apparent "determinism" such mathematically exact physical laws seem to imply. He may not always have held this insight firmly in his sights, however, for he still occasionally expresses himself as though these "determinisms" still held true for physical realities themselves, and were both "respected" and "employed" by the higher synthesizing power of "life" (compare chap. 5, note 17, above). Thoroughgoing consistency would have encouraged the flat-out affirmation that determinisms are uniformly illusory, even at the atomic and infra-atomic levels: all Matter is "pre-living," and thereby endowed with some faint modicum of "within" and therefore some minimal spontaneity. By the time he writes PM, his thought will have acquired the firmer consistency which warrants his making that bold generalization.

mined insistence that humanity represents a cosmic novelty in "absolute" terms. Teilhard does not dwell on the resolution of this anomaly in his "Hominization" essay; but later developments will show it could not have been far from his thoughts.

8

Crisis and Faith:
In Evolution

IN HIS "HOMINIZATION" ESSAY, written in 1925, Teilhard makes an early allusion to the "crisis" he sees evolution passing through during our "modern" age of history. The "problem of action" with which that crisis confronts present-day humanity had been, we know, the subject of lengthy conversations, particularly with Jean Boussac, during the agonizing months they spent together at the Front during the First World War.[1] Boussac envisaged the past stages of evolution as moving majestically forward, its individual elements subordinated to the upward march of life as a whole—until, that is, humanity came on the scene.

For from that moment, a reversal was possible, and this "dirty war" showed clearly that the reversal had occurred; individual self-consciousness and egoistic self-centeredness had seized control of the process. For the first time in all of natural history as we know it, the evolutionary "element" could claim individual rights, not only against the human species, but against the entire evolutionary process of which humanity was part and product.[2] Humanity, evolution's finest achievement, could assume the stance of questioner and critic toward the evolutionary "womb" which brought it forth; humanity alone could consciously measure and freely reject the demands of self-subordina-

[1] See *The Making of a Mind: Letters from a Soldier-Priest, 1914–1919*, trans. René Hague (New York: Harper & Row, 1965), pp. 103–24, for Teilhard's report of these continued discussions with Boussac.

[2] Here begins my summary of Teilhard's analysis of humanity's present situation; see VP 74–76/105–108.

tion which the survival and advance of the species imposed. The human individual could, first among earth's living forms, stare straight at the death which inevitably ends all earthly life, and refuse to "go gently" into that night to which all pre-human life-forms unreflectively and unprotestingly submit. Self-abnegation and death: these twin evils are the coinage each element must consent to pay in if evolution is to progress. But never until evolution had become "hominized" and self-reflective, had "evil" become a conscious and anguishing "problem." For the very first time, the evolutionary element was in a position to "revolt" against the requirements of evolutionary success—to revolt, or, simply, to "go on strike."

Revolts and strikes, Teilhard observes, can take a variety of forms: paroxysms of individual self-isolation; desperate efforts, frantic and doomed, to break out of our cosmic "prison"; or the softer road of self-intoxication through drink or drugs or pleasure—they are all one in sharing the same lack of "faith and courage." We need courage to live up to evolution's often stark demands on us; but even more fundamentally, we need "faith" in the "supreme value of evolution" and in the "magnificent cause" which it embodies.

It is important to grasp exactly, once and for all, the kind of "faith" to which Teilhard is summoning his readers, here, in 1925, and, later on as well, in *The Phenomenon of Man*. It is question of a faith in "evolution" as representing both a "supreme value" and a "cause" magnificent enough to enlist our most valiant human efforts. There is not the slightest whisper, at this stage of his argument, of a "supernatural" or specifically Christian faith. Granted: there is a vaguely religious tone in the way Teilhard speaks of "evolution" as value and cause; but Teilhard is convinced that such a tone is justified once his reader takes seriously the "more distinct and realistic" picture of evolution's grandeur and scope he has coached that reader's eyes to "see."

And that vision, in all its aspects, he reminds us at the close of this early essay, resposes on the "purely experimental level." In fact, the only juncture at which he consents to leave that phenomenal level sees him chiding those patrons of a "spiritual" morality who deprecate all evolutionary views as seeds of purely materialistic values and universal conflict. To them he points out that their Christian faith implicitly recognizes the Incarnate Christ as the continuing influence battling against the individualistic egoism, selfish quest for pleasure, evasion of responsibility, and rejection of self-transcending abnegation which threaten the vital success of evolution; there is, therefore, a profound consonance between evolutionary and Christian ethical demands (VP 76–79/108–11). But this is precisely what his fellow-Christians fail to see, the reason being that they either fail or refuse to take the natural, the human, the evolutionary, with appropriate natural and human seriousness. Teilhard's complaint, when addressing his "audience" of fellow-Christians, is constant and consistent from first to last: they must first become "human" enough to rethink their Christianity in terms which resonate powerfully with the needs and legitimate aspirations of their fellow-humans, the all-too-frequently alienated "builders of the earth."

This point, though scarcely recondite, seems totally to have eluded the mind of George Gaylord Simpson. One would have expected from him, a world expert on evolutionary theory and a personal acquaintance of Teilhard's, a careful understanding of *The Phenomenon of Man*. But when Simpson exultantly discovers Teilhard appealing to modern man for this "act of faith," he vaults to the conclusion that it is the very act of Christian faith which Teilhard had smuggled into the vision of evolution he has presented to us, from the first page of his work until now. His claim, therefore, of having conducted his argument on the purely "scientific" level, a claim which Simpson equally misconstrues, was, after all, less than "honest."[3]

Now, the most cursory examination of the context shows up Simpson's logic as that of a somewhat sorry amateur. Teilhard is appealing for an act of faith—that much is clear—but a purely human act of faith, quite demonstrably not the theological and Christian act of faith which did, in fact, sustain his earlier and later overtly religious exposés of the Christic dimension of evolution. But in those exposés, he makes it abundantly clear that he is writing in another genre, and arguing on a different level from the genre and level which characterizes *The Phenomenon of Man* or, more precisely for the purposes of this study, the "vision of the past" encased in that work.

Faced with the modern world's unease before the discovery of evolutionary space–time, Teilhard expands his "Hominization" argument by pointing out that modern mankind is confronted with a dilemma and a choice: "either nature," having evolved as far as mankind, is "closed" to the human demand for fulfillment, so that its finest product turns out to be "stifled and stillborn" in a universe both "self-abortive and absurd"; or some "opening" does exist, some "way out" toward the "unlimited psychic spaces" for which thought, once born, inevitably yearns. In this latter case, we live in a "universe to which we can unhesitatingly entrust ourselves." Given the way the human psyche is built, Teilhard argues, there is neither "middle road" nor "halfway house"; the road before us runs either up or down, toward hope or ultimate despair. And now we come to the appeal on which Simpson so triumphantly pounced: "Neither on one side nor on the other is there any piece of tangible evidence. But, for hop-

---

[3] See his review, cited in the Introduction, note 2.

ing [rather than despairing], there are rational invitations
to making an act of faith" (PM 233/258).

What are those "rational invitations"? In answer to that,
Teilhard replies both early and late, in 1940 as in 1925,
by summing up his view of the "whole world" seen as a
single natural history, inexorably rising, juggling so "mi-
raculously" and "infallibly" with all sorts of improbabili-
ties until, in the end, it begot humanity. What "risk" can
there be in "committing ourselves further, and following"
the work of evolution "right to the end"? If evolution took
up the work, it can "bring it to completion," and do so by
"following the same methods, and with the same infallibility, as it brought to its beginnings" (PM 233–34/258–
59; cf. VP 77–79/110–11[4]).

Now, this supposes a great deal: that we have accepted
the "vision of the past" Teilhard has thus far presented to
us. If we have, then there are grounds for "entrusting" ourselves to the kind of world he has sketched for us, for believing and hoping that the future promises us some form
or other of "continuation" and "survival," some "superior
form of existence" we shall reach if only we "think and walk
in the direction" which evolution may be counted on to
take in its continual progress.

But "some form or other" of "continuation" and "survival," some "superior form of existence"—there is nothing *specifically* Christian here. And *pace* Simpson, our
acceptance of the "vision of the past" Teilhard has been
presenting up to this stage in his argument is logically independent of whether we are willing to entrust ourselves
further to the workings of the kind of world he has pre-

---

[4] There is a suggestive difference between these two treatments, however.
Writing for himself, and for an imaginary audience which obviously included
believing Christians resistant to the notion of evolution, the earlier Teilhard
interweaves both scientific and theological argumentation; writing a scientific
mémoire, however (as was his claim in PM), he is careful to eliminate any
such appeal to Christian belief.

sented for our acceptance. Logically, it all depends on whether Teilhard has marshaled and illumined the "evidence" cogently enough to prompt us to "see" the entire process of evolution as a coordinated upthrust of psychism toward greater consciousness and liberty—and life. The human act of faith in evolution's promise of an even richer future for us does not logically subtend this vision of the past, but plainly depends upon and follows from it as an action corollary. The cogency of the vision, therefore, can and must be judged on the merits of the argument and evidence as Teilhard has tried to "light it" for our eyes.

Simpson would have been closer to the mark in pointing to a philosophic premiss implied in Teilhard's argument at this precise juncture. For, like his contemporary Blondel, Teilhard was convinced that the law inscribed in all human activity was this: no truly self-reflective being does anything except out of the conviction (however dimly avowed or unanalyzed it may remain) that he or she is doing something valuable, that its value is enduring, and that something of it will remain forever. Convince a self-reflective being that the results of all his efforts, though they may endure for thousands of millennia, will ultimately be wiped away *entirely* leaving "not a wrack behind," and that being will soon perceive that this reduces the value of any single achievement exactly to zero. Postponements, however indefinite, will not attenuate the absurdity of undertaking any effort under such conditions; if the end result is zero, then the thing is of no worth whatever, and the person with only a glimmer of lucidity will either revolt or go on strike.

Now, it might be fairly argued that the reasoning here is philosophical; it could conceivably be further argued that it is unconvincing. But it certainly cannot be convincingly argued, as Simpson does, that Teilhard is here surreptitiously inviting us to make an act of Christian faith, or that he is even drawing *this precise conviction* from the Christian faith which did, in the last resort, sustain his personal life.

For Christians of his time did not necessarily feel, as Teilhard did, this need for affirming the eternal value of human activity. As Christians they all too frequently took the pose of standing fastidiously aside from all the world's concerns, of looking with sanctimonious suspicion on the giant task of research and advancement which the "world-lings" all about them were engaged in. If Teilhard bends every effort to prove to his co-religionists the value of human activity, and does so by taking his stance formally on the Christian message, he must first of all stress aspects of that message which he was convinced had drifted out of focus; must harp again and again on strands in Sts. John and Paul whose cosmic impact was largely ignored by exegetes of his time (and is even left in shadow by some today); must write a *Divine Milieu* which in the end was refused publication by Catholicism's highest officialdom. Even at present, despite Vatican II, it is still possible for Christians to feel that human activity is just so much "bas-ket-weaving," passing the time from now until death, its products destined to vanish utterly when this world passes away; the eternity spoken of in Christianity is not, for this sort of mentality, the guarantee of the worth of our human task, but something much closer to the opposite.

It was not, therefore, the Christianity which was taught him which made Teilhard believe in the undying value of human activity, including scientific research. It was precisely his antecedent conviction of its value which impelled him to rethink the shape of the Christianity which had been taught him, giving it a cast both ancient and new. Nor was it the Christian faith precisely as it had been taught him which persuaded him to "entrust himself" to the world; *that* Christianity would have counseled just the opposite. Rather, it was his spontaneous, personal attraction, which he was persuaded was both "natural" and "human," toward the "heart of matter" which prompted him to distrust those voices which urged him to turn away from the world in order to seek the Christian God. But then he found himself obliged to search the Scriptures in order to see whether Christianity was as opposed to his natural attraction as those voices claimed.[5]

In sum, if Teilhard appeals in *The Phenomenon of Man* for an "act of faith," it is for an act of faith he considers indispensable for the "natural" man as such; the same act of faith he had made quite early in his life, and one which seemed *at first* to come in conflict with his Christianity; an act of faith *in the world*. And if he went to the enormous task of building a "vision of the past," it was with the intention of getting us, Christians or otherwise, first of all to be *human*. He meant to present us with the grounds for making an act of faith "in the world," a faith he thought especially needed at this juncture of evolutionary development.

Examined logically, therefore, the objection we have been considering turns out to seem worthless: the act of faith Teilhard invites us to make cannot be turned into an incrimination of the vision of the past which has preceded, and which (in his eyes) grounds that act of faith. In fact, viewed against the background of Teilhard's personal development, that plea for faith argues rather for than against his "honesty."

But Simpson's objection could have been put in more careful form, a form which would lend it greater validity. The Teilhard he came to know, the mature Teilhard, had already come to terms with the problem of Christianity and evolution, had already succeeded in forging the coincidence between those two "hearts" of his boyhood religious experience—the heart of matter and the heart of Christ.

---

[5] See the title essay in HM on this set of tensions and its meaning in Teilhard's own development.

He was living on a faith which was no longer merely a faith in the world, but one for which the *Christ-Evoluteur* had, by His Incarnation and Redemption, penetrated to the depths of the evolving real. Christ, Teilhard loved to repeat, had pronounced the words "This is My Body" over the entire material cosmos, and was now leavening its advance toward the Fullness of His Body, the Pleroma spoken of by St. Paul. The Christian Mystery was not, therefore, something apart from, irrelevant to, the world revealed to us by phenomenological investigation. True, he warns repeatedly that the sources of our knowledge of the Mystery remain forever distinct from, never to be "confused" with, the sources and methods whereby we gain knowledge of the phenomenal real; and yet, they both speak of the same objective world: their messages must "converge" even if they do not become confused. By virtue of the form he had given his personal Christianity, Teilhard's theological act of faith is in a Christ Who has become Heart of the evolving world; and by that same token, his "human" act of faith is in a world in which, for his consciousness, the Risen Christ is tirelessly at work. He has brought the Christian vision into powerful resonance with his human vision of the world; more than likely, then, the strength and serenity of his "natural" faith in the world was powerfully abetted by that resonance. For a consciousness as unitary as his, the problem of keeping these two visions from becoming "confused" while still allowing them to "converge" must always have been a delicate one. At this point the question may, and must, be asked: To what extent did Teilhard's fully articulated Christian vision of the world exercise a subtle influence on his faith in the future, and, indirectly, on his vision of the past?

Let me put that question more concretely. Teilhard would trace the shape of the future by following, and projecting forward, the lines of evolution out of the past and through the present. The "Hominization" essay pre-

sents us with an early, but remarkably formed, envisagement of the present state of evolution: the elaboration of
what he terms the "organic unity" of humanity. Having
discarded the absolute distinction between the biologically
"natural" and the humanly "artificial," he enumerates the
"artificial" linkages which humanity has forged for itself,
but in such a way as to bring out their natural, biological
value; they constitute a veritable "nervous system" for a
humanity which can be considered, not metaphorically,
but analogically, as an "organism." For the human envelope is bonded into one by juridical and social bonds,
assuredly; and yet, eliminate the artificial–natural distinction, and those bonds become natural, physical, and biological. Still, it remains just as true that the unity of the
human "organism" is being forged "clearly in the psychological domain"; the physical and biological have been
thoroughly "hominized" in their mode of operation. The
result is that this bonding, unlike that of the many cells in
our bodily organism, goes on "without the suppression of
individuals" and of their individuality (VP 59–60/80).

Now, this is a striking paradox: the unity and progressive unification of *this* peculiar organism does *not* result
in the suppression of the individuality—the individual consciousness and freedom—of the member-parts, as so many
of Teilhard's rapid-reader critics have complained it must.
His claim, in fact, is quite the reverse: that this precise sort
of unification succeeds in actually *enhancing* the "differ-
entiation" of the personalities who consciously and freely
consent to the "mega-synthesis"—not merely the "forced
coalescence"—which is currently underway in our evolving world.[6]

---

[6] Too little attention has been paid to this capital distinction. Teilhard sees
"forced coalescence" as inevitable, given (among other factors) the growth
of population on the limited surface of our planet; but it can be transformed
into that quite different reality, genuine "mega-synthesis," only through the
willing intervention of love (see PM 239–45/265–72). Indeed, Teilhard's
motivation in writing PM was to coach humanity to see the indispensability of

Such an organism, however, strikes the mind as quite peculiar. Not only peculiar, Teilhard replies. It is unique, incomparable; no other organic whole in our experience would have given us an exact idea of it. Where, then, did Teilhard get the idea? The Epilogue to *The Phenomenon of Man* answers that question with disarming candor. There he describes the vision of Christ's Fullness in the light of Sts. Paul and John, a Fullness toward which the world is striving in virtue of a Christ Who has become the "principle of universal vitality," working to "purify, to direct, and to superanimate the general ascent of consciousness into which He inserted Himself." Central to the image which he traces out is the notion of "God, the Center of centers"— preserving and enhancing our individualities in the very act of "communion and sublimation" which one would have expected to "suppress" them. "So perfectly does this coincide with the Omega Point" which his hyperphysical vision of reality requires, Teilhard admits, that "doubtless I should never have ventured to envisage" that Omega Point, or "formulate the hypothesis rationally if I had not found, in my consciousness as a believer, not only its speculative model but also its living reality" (PM 294/328).

Again, the man's candor is disarming. "I might," he has already avowed, "be suspected of wanting to introduce an apologia by artifice. But here again, so far as it is possible for a man to separate in himself the various planes of knowledge, it is not the convinced believer but the naturalist who is asking for a hearing" (PM 292/325). Here, then, is Simpson's objection once again, but put into a form more refined and cogent than Simpson was able to devise for it. "So far as it is possible for a man to separate in himself the various planes of knowledge": the wording itself is

---

making this "great option"; compare PM 232–34/258–59 with "The Phenomenon of Man" in FM 37–60/55–81. Rabut, *Teilhard de Chardin*, elides this vital point, making one wonder why Teilhard thought it important to persuade us of his views in the first place.

implicit admission that the "separation" is psychologically demanding, and that no man ever knows for certain how far he has succeeded in achieving it. How far did his faith envisagement of the Christic Fullness "key" Teilhard's hyperphysical envisagement of the dominant lines of present-day humanity's tendency toward "organic unity"? And, then, how far did that envisagement light up the dominant lines of past history in such a way as to show them as groping toward the shape of present-day humanity?

Logically, Teilhard's projection of humanity's future depends upon the accuracy with which he has portrayed the past as generating the present. From this, the logical point of view, Simpson's objection can easily be discarded. But psychologically it is truer to say that Teilhard was looking at the past from the vantage point of the future, rather than the reverse. Rephrased in terms of this psychology of discovery, then, Simpson's objection becomes at once more refined and telling. But then, proving its validity becomes a far more refined and demanding business than he dreamed.

For Teilhard's reference to the Pauline Pleroma as the "speculative model" which brought him to envisage the evolutionary process along the lines he did was calculated to give the reflective scientist pause; perhaps this is why Professor Simpson avoided citing the passage where Teilhard makes this admission. For the scientist who has thought a bit about the way science works knows well that it is a matter of relative indifference where one goes to find one's "speculative models." Who would have thought that what astronomy tells us of the solar system could have become—initially at least—useful as a "speculative model" suggesting the inner workings of the atom? The value of the "model" consists in its sharpening of the observer's eye for tricks and folds of the reality to be observed; it gets us to interrogate that reality in fresh, sometimes previously unimagined ways; it provokes us to look for properties which no one ever before thought of finding there, much less of finding at all significant. If the properties dictated by the model are, by careful observation, found in the reality, then the model has served its initial purpose; it has shown itself, up to a point at least, to be a serviceable analogue of the reality, and to that extent an inviting lead toward eventual "natural classification" in Duhem's sense. What the scientist must ask is whether the properties have been truly "found"; it does not occur to him to conclude, without conscientious examination, that the "speculative model" just *put* them there. Simpson may well have seen that had he aimed his objection from this vantage point, it would have put the onus on him of showing in detail that the properties Teilhard claimed to have "found" in phenomenal reality were simply not "there" to be found, or were other than he claimed.

Or, in a more primitive language: the model suggests a significant "pattern" in terms of which the "facts" may be observed and subsequently brought into some intelligible order. Complain about the choice of model, and you must make your objection stick by grappling with the facts, showing that they have been distorted, deformed, invented, or submitted to some such process of falsification, by having been envisaged in the light cast by the "wrongly chosen" speculative model.

But even that way of putting it is, I repeat, a trifle primitive—too primitive for handling the case before us. Again, Teilhard has anticipated the objection. There are no pure "facts" in science; every single observation made supposes in the very making of it an entire web of theoretical assumptions; the "facts" observed are themselves already caught up, and to some extent formed, by the crisscross lighting of theory. Fifty years of personal scientific activity have only confirmed in Teilhard's mind the validity of Duhem's insistence on that truth. True for science in its more ordinary journeyman operations, though, this difficulty is raised to the third or fourth power when it is question of proposing and testing a "total" theory. Present a scientist with a new way of envisaging the world as a whole, from top to bottom, and immediately you are asking him to see the "facts" as taking on a radically new configuration; to accord importance to features which before he had hardly stopped to notice; to look for "dominant lines" in the cosmic landscape which he was viewing before in terms of dominants entirely, or markedly, different. For that reason, the somewhat simplistic language which would portray the scientist as first erecting a "model," then "looking for the facts," does not work when it comes to doing justice to that "supreme spiritual act" of hypothetic envisagement which bodies itself forth in observations which, far from being logically subsequent, antiseptically neutral "second steps," are really its organic prolongations.

Once the central "scientific act" is viewed this way, not as a dry step-by-step logical process, but as a psychologically complex work of the creative imagination operating at the height of its powers, it becomes obvious how much refinement and delicacy must be brought to the business of making such an objection as Simpson's "stick." Teilhard's view of reality, like any revolutionary hypothesis, asks us to stare, not at an assemblage of brute isolable "facts," but rather at a system of relations, shadings, dominants, dynamics; it invites us to redistribute areas of importance in ways we find strange and initially shocking—as strange and shocking as their hearers found Copernicus' proposal, or Darwin's, or Freud's. Teilhard is asking us to don the thinking cap he wove for his own head over years, use his eyes as our spectacles, look, and wait, look again and wait to see whether the entire landscape (given time) comes finally into focus.

It must also be recognized that the kind of "certainty" involved in such a noetic act is of a special sort. It is far from the type so common in Greek thought: inspect a genuinely intelligible connection, and its truth will become as evident and indubitable to you as the mathematical connection of 7, 3, and 10. Nor is it the type of that mythically "pure" empirical certainty which the observer is fancied to enjoy if he simply focuses on some atomic "fact." In the second case, the story goes, he cannot doubt "what's simply *so*"; in the first, "what's *necessarily* so." The certainty Teilhard offers is of a more demanding and unstable sort; it might usefully be compared to the certainty which a slightly color-blind man might have, after the hints and finger-tracings of a healthy-eyed companion have aided him to "see" on the color-blind chart the patterns which previously escaped him. The illustration would be slightly more (though far from perfectly) exact if one supposed that such "practice" in detection could actually remedy color-blindness; and further, that the previous condition of his eye had led him to see, not merely a jumble, but another pattern entirely—one which may even have been there, but turns out now to have been far less satisfying and compelling than the new one he is led to discern.

For *discernment* is the word which best translates the act of mind Teilhard is asking us to execute; and discernment is an active, creative operation, more delicate, demanding, and less peremptory in its claims to furnish apodictic "evidence" than mathematics and "pure" empiricism are happy with. Of this kind of "seeing" the Husserlian dictum pre-eminently holds: no man can be brought to see what he refuses to see.

Which brings us back, but now for a final time, to Simpson's objection: Teilhard was certainly predisposed by the personal form he had given his Christian faith to "see" in the past the development which he saw leading to a human present, that human present in its turn already illumined by a Pauline view of the ultimate future. He saw, one may say, what he was "willing" to see.

But to what extent did his "willingness" lead him to accentuate certain relationships rather than others; place a stress on unity, analogy, and wholeness which was just that shade too heavy; discern as dominants what really are relatively secondary lines of structure or dynamism—in short, redistribute importance in the infinitely subtle way a master pianist would do, who wished to play a Mozart piece with convincing fidelity and still suggest a Mozart already prefiguring the early Beethoven?

This, I submit, is the way Simpson's objection might better have been put. And put that way, it has no answer. Or, if you will, we can never know the answer, any more than Teilhard himself did or could. For if his playing of scientific Mozart sounds to some like theological Beethoven, the influence of Beethoven worked largely in the "tacit dimension." Moreover, enough has been written on the question to suggest from other angles what this study only serves to confirm: there were few things Teilhard detested more than the small-minded self-deceptions which went into writing that classic genre, the "apologia by artifice," no matter what cause the "apologia" was intended to serve. His largeness of spirit made him, if anything, only more impatient with that form of writing when it was done in the interests of the Christianity he desired so much to serve.

But "apologies" are of many sorts. The fact that the term "apologetics" has found a place in the classic lexicon of Christian theology should not blind us to the truth that there is a genre of anti-Christian, anti-theist "apologetics" as well, and that much of it may operate as unconsciously (or consciously) by "artifice" as certain of his critics have insinuated about Teilhard. Why is it we suspect an "apologetic" intent wherever the real is claimed to rhyme with theism or Christianity, whereas, when reality is shown to be "absurd," "entropic," totally out of tune with all men's dreams and aspirations, we are far more given to speak of austere, sober objectivity? It may just be possible that his "willingness" to see was the needed psychological condition for Teilhard's actually seeing what was *there*; and that his critics may at times usefully ask whether their consciences are quite so clear on the matter as his seems to have been.

In any event, the objection that his Christian faith led him to distort the lines of the real is as easy to make as it is impossible to make stick. The ease with which it can be made is feeble grounds indeed for approaching his "vision of the past" with hostile suspicions; it deserves to be judged as it stands, and on its merits. And if there is any interest in that judgment's being made objectively, there are at least minor advantages in having read, and in having attempted to understand, Teilhard's own thoughts—not thoughts which we, to make him easier to deal with, have chosen to put in his head.

But does this mean that there are no difficulties whatever, no questionable passages of logic, in Teilhard's "vision" of the past? By no means. We must deal with them at the proper time.

9

The Phenomenon of Man:
A Scientific *Mémoire*

THERE MAY BE GAPS IN THIS SURVEY of how Teilhard elaborated, step by step, the "vision of the past" he eventually encased in *The Phenomenon of Man*; but we may be reasonably confident that those gaps cannot be very large ones. For a close reading of *The Phenomenon of Man* will show, I submit, that by 1928 its author had come to express every major facet of the hypothesis and method which he eventually applied in that work of synthesis.[1]

What we have seen to this point warns us, however, that *The Phenomenon of Man* requires, and I would add deserves, a closer reading than it has all too frequently been given; a carefully composed book, it will yield its message only to an equally careful reading.

Consider, for example, the guidelines Teilhard explicitly sets out for the proper understanding of his work, first in its Preface (PM 29–30/21–23), then in its Foreword (PM 31–36/25–30).[2] He will have it read, he warns

---

[1] It might be argued that the bold attack on the myth of the scientist as purely objective spectator, penned in 1936 (see HE 54–55/70–71), represents a radical advance on the views of scientific activity embodied in the essays written from 1920 to 1928. We shall come to that question farther on; my own view is that it is more a consistent prolongation of than a departure from Teilhard's earlier views.

Another insight which rises to greater prominence after 1928 focuses on the importance of the "round earth" as constituting a "closed volume" which, like the closed volume of a sealed kettle, prevents the indefinite expansion-dissipation of mounting energy "pressures"; but this, I submit, is more an application of the critical threshold idea than a truly novel discovery.

Both these questions are strictly historical ones, however, and may remain secondary to the argument of this study.

[2] The following pages are a paraphrase of these two sections of the work,

the reader, "uniquely and exclusively as a scientific *mé-moire*." The current English translation does him the disservice of translating *mémoire* as "treatise"; had Teilhard wished to say that, he would have used the term *traité*, and a number of critics would have had initial justification, at least, for concluding that he claimed to be writing "science" in the technical and currently accepted form of that genre. But even with that mistranslation working against him, a fair-minded critic would have been brought up short by the added remarks Teilhard makes in order to situate the level on which he is pitching his work.

For Teilhard goes on to specify his work in terms of what it is *not*: the claim that it moves on the scientific level is meant to exclude the suspicion that it is a work of "metaphysics" or even of "theology." Clearly, he expects such suspicions to arise, for the very "total" character of the synthesis he is about to present inevitably makes any such work "look like" what it is not, can "give the impression" of being a philosophy or a theology. He illustrates this by comparing his work with those of an Einstein, a Poincaré, or a Jeans. Here again, the careful reader is being warned: all three men wrote strictly "scientific" treatises in their fields, but alongside those conventionally acceptable scientific contributions, Teilhard expects them to be known to us for their larger, more ambitious attempts to spell out the total picture of our universe which their scientific activity eventually prompted them to propose: not "treatises," but "*mémoires*."

Consider Sir James Jeans in this connection. Alongside his technical treatises on gases and thermodynamics, he ventured to publish such well-known works, more synthetic and popular in compass and tone, as *The Universe Around Us*. To this precise work Teilhard refers in a letter written

---

executed in the light which Teilhard's progressive, and more expanded earlier, statements shed on the highly condensed prose of PM.

in 1931;[3] he has read and found it, for all its assurances to the contrary, a scientific gospel of despair. The universe beheld by the reflective physicist is doomed, says Jeans; but let not our hearts be troubled, the day of doom is still far off. But Teilhard's central criticism of Jeans is suggestive in the extreme: he has not shown any just appreciation of the "phenomenon" represented by "life" in our universe. In other words, his work is flawed even on the "scientific" level.

For this is what Teilhard means by a *mémoire* which remains genuinely scientific: it takes its premises and chooses its evidence uniquely from observation—*expériment*—of phenomenal reality. It neither supposes as its premises nor launches into any speculations concerning the "causal relationships" or "essence of being" which the metaphysician claims to discover "underlying" the connections and workings of phenomenal reality. A writer of a scientific *mémoire* will neither affirm nor deny the usefulness of such metaphysical exploration;[4] he will leave room for it as another angle of approach to the real than his own; he may fancy that his findings about the phenomenal real provide some grist for the metaphysician's mill, but he will sedulously refrain from making any venture into metaphysics, and *a fortiori* into theology, precisely (as Duhem had long ago insisted) in order to safeguard the autonomy of the theory he is about to present on experimental grounds, accessible to all and sundry who are simply willing to make the requisite observations.

But this very canon Teilhard has been accused of violating, and more than once. We saw how ill-directed Simpson's accusation was in this connection; but Toulmin has

[3] See the letter of May 4, 1931, in *Letters from a Traveller* (London: Collins, 1962), p. 176.

[4] Etienne Gilson said it well somewhere: denying the value of metaphysics is itself a metaphysical claim. Duhem and Teilhard were far more alert to that than many of their critics.

brought a similar charge by claiming that Teilhard was writing "natural theology," and even so friendly a critic as Dobzhansky claims to find poetry, mysticism, and metaphysics in Teilhard's work. The study just concluded on the genesis of his method, however, poses a number of questions to such charges. Before advancing on those questions, though, let me repeat the main and precise contention presiding over this study: I am focusing exclusively on the "vision of the past" which Teilhard presents in Parts I and II, and in the first two chapters of Part III of *The Phenomenon of Man*. That vision of the past, I would claim, is logically independent for its cogency and evidential quality of whatever "metaphysics" or even "mysticism" one may claim to uncover in later sections of the work. Here, I suggest, Toulmin has put it rightly: the seriousness we bring to Teilhard's recommendations concerning future lines of human action must spring from the correctness we find in his vision of the past, and that vision of the past may and must be evaluated on its own merits. Evaluated that way, finally, I consider Teilhard has presented a serious case for claiming that his vision of the evolutionary past is indeed *based*, not on any metaphysics, much less on any mysticism or theology, "natural" or otherwise, but on a highly sophisticated survey of "experimental" evidence.

We have seen how the French connotations of that term "experimental," reinforced by his own experience and method as a paleontologist, entitled Teilhard to a more extended understanding of the expression than an English-speaking physicist or chemist might countenance, or even accept as valid. We have also seen, however, the grounds for Teilhard's growing conviction that Newtonian physics could stake only shaky claims to posing as the model and norm for how "scientific" activity was supposed to be conducted. In fact, implicit in his hypothesis is the reverse of that contention: the superstitious idolatry of physics is precisely what contributes to the scientist's inveterate tendency to *ignore* those psychic properties and activities which are more directly knowable and more certainly known to us as human beings than virtually anything we know about material reality.

One may, if one chooses, quarrel with that contention; the quarrel, Teilhard would claim, would arise from a too simplistic and unreflectively dogmatic notion of what "science" is, and should be, about. His grounds for making that further contention we have already examined; in any event, one cannot take the first step in sympathetic understanding of *The Phenomenon of Man* without first granting him this much: that the "psychic" is a "phenomenon," and since it is such, the scientist has no valid grounds for excluding it from his observations and synthetic statements about the entirety of the observable real.

But even granting this, the conscientious scientific thinker might object: psychic properties and activities may be object of direct observation "within" our human selves; the paleontologist, furthermore, may be entitled to infer the activity of psychism from the exterior evidence of tools, fire, and artifacts; but does this give us grounds for claiming that such psychic properties are verifiable in animals, plants, or even on the level of atomic and molecular matter? Verifiable, directly observable? No, Teilhard replies. But indirectly ascertainable in a way quite similar to the way science, in its conventionally accepted procedure even now, claims to ascertain the existence of certain atomic particles or astronomical bodies? This is quite another matter, and no reflective scientist should be surprised to hear the question re-formed this way, and answered in these more refined terms.

For the moment, however, Teilhard considers it premature to "prove" the existence of a psychic "within" on every level of material reality. So, for the present, he calls our attention to it as an "assumption" undergirding his entire synthesis.

He calls our attention to a second major assumption: that humanity may and must be regarded as a "whole," and, indeed, as a whole in the "organic" sense of that term; not merely a collection of disparate individuals, humanity may and must be seen as a biological unity, very much[5] on the model of a single anatomical individual.

We have seen how Teilhard came in time to develop these two "assumptions" as more than merely that; they are, he is convinced, the two major methodological keys required for "saving science"—science, that is, as implicitly aspiring to a single, total "natural history" of the phenomenal real, a Duhemian "natural classification." But there was a privileged locus in the web of phenomena where the need of these two methodological keys came most urgently into view: that locus was the human group, and the anomalies encountered when science tries to "place" humanity correctly. It could be argued that this is the point at which Teilhard could usefully have begun the argument of *The Phenomenon of Man*; but, as it stands, the focal treatment of the human group occurs much later in the book, only after he has given his exposé of the "natural history" of the earth, and life, and pre-human living beings, all supposing the two "assumptions" whose grounding becomes plainest and most compelling once they are glimpsed as imposed by the anomalies involved in "classifying" humanity "scientifically."

Whatever one thinks of this compositional strategy, it imposes certain requirements on Teilhard and on his reader; the two major insights he could so swiftly justify when

[5] Not *exactly* on this model, be it noted; Teilhard is keenly aware of the "corrections for analogy" required up and down the levels of evolutionary reality. See Henri de Lubac's instructive study of this facet of Teilhard's thinking in *The Religion of Teilhard de Chardin*, trans. René Hague (New York: Desclee, 1967), pp. 189–94.

writing his earlier essays on "Hominization" and "The Phenomenon of Man" must wait in the wings for their justification in this work, all the while commanding the development of the argument from its very first stages.

Hence, the need Teilhard experiences for stating these assumptions at the very outset; hence, too, the need for reminding his reader repeatedly[6] that they are at work, and receive their more explicit justification only at the stage when the human group discloses itself as the "rent" or "breach," in and through which this organic and psychic character of the whole skein of "natural history" is most compellingly glimpsed. Meanwhile, we must grant him the right to anticipate on what humanity tells us about our universe, and take the human group as the "center" of this entire construction.

Hence, finally, the need Teilhard now experiences to remind us of how such a "total theory" must be tested. For in any total theory, the "whole" is present and presupposed in every one of its parts. Instead of howling imprecations about "vicious circles," therefore, one must respect the peculiar logical demands involved in the elaboration of all total theories and, reserving judgment, wait until the theory has been totally unfolded. At that point, and no sooner, the appropriate question is the familiar Duhemian one: does this theory, in its totality and in all its interdependent parts, show forth the "coherent order," the "coherence and homogeneity," which declares it a genuinely "natural classification" of the observable real? Or, in more "natural historical" terms: does it succeed in establishing—or, better, uncovering—the order in which observable consequents follow upon their observable antecedents, an order which comes down to a set of "laws of recurrence" which oper-

---

[6] Reminders occur with almost tiresome frequency. See, for example, PM 39–40, 47, 54, 62, 79, 82–83, 85, 88–89, 112, 146, 153, 160, 166, 180/34, 41, 50, 59, 79, 84, 86, 91, 92, 119, 158, 167, 174, 182, 198, as well as PM 70/68, though here the reminder is slightly masked under Wall's imprecise translation.

ate on every level of the phenomenal real, from atom to humanity?

Coherence and homogeneity: but of a theory which is at every step in its elaboration obedient to the "facts." But what are "the facts"? Here Teilhard warns his reader away from the naïvetés of an unreflective positivism which would claim that there are scientific "facts" in some pure form, irresistible atoms of evidence entirely independent of the all-encompassing web of theory in which they are undivorceably enmeshed. Enmeshed in scientists' theories, the "facts" are for that very reason unavoidably affected by scientists' subjectivities; the totally "objective" scientific fact is another outworn myth. Let no one accuse Teilhard of being "unscientific," then, for allowing his personal subjectivity to influence the point of vantage and lines of priority which govern the style of observation he employs in this work; every scientist does the same whether wittingly or no.[7] And when the theory is "total," as this one is, the synthesizer's subjectivity, if always legitimately, responsibly, and correctly brought into play, both may and must be expected to exercise a dominant role. The question for science is, not the elimination, but the proper employment, of subjectivity. For only a subjectivity properly attuned can ever be truly "objective," and hope to catch the sinuous curvings of reality.

Or, put in the familiar terms he uses in his Foreword: only the properly educated "eye" can be expected to "see" what is truly there. But even the properly educated eye must take up its position at the correct vantage point—which means, in this case, focusing on humanity as the central, the most significant and revealing, clue to the way in which our evolving world has been "constructed." Anthro-

---

[7] See the bold statement on this referred to in note 1 above. Teilhard may have been encouraged in this direction by advances in atomic physics which eventually led to, among other things, Werner Heisenberg's "indeterminacy principle." But his relative isolation in Peking at this time makes it difficult to measure his acquaintance with those developments.

pocentrism: Teilhard indirectly reminds his readers of how suspicious modern science has always been of that posture. Scientists must acknowledge, of course, that every observer is necessarily the *subjective* center *from which* all observations have to be made. But post-Renaissance science, in its unremitting quest for some kind of pure "objectivity," has struggled tirelessly to break free of this "bondage" to subjectivity. It has bent every effort toward producing that totally detached "spectator" whose subjectivity becomes so completely effaced as not in the least to alter or distort the message of "phenomena in themselves." Alas, the progress of science has demonstrated the quixotic vanity of such a hope. Teilhard goes back to the problem which Duhem, Poincaré, and others had highlighted decades earlier: we now realize that the most "objective" observations of all scientists are so shot through with the conventions and forms of thought which have grown up with the growth of science that the burning question now is whether scientific constructions are commanded by the shape of the realities being studied or are merely the "reflection of [scientists'] own ways of thinking."

But that is not all. The scientist's study of "outside" reality has brought him to realize that he himself is an integral element *in* that reality; the evolutionary construction he once thought of putting on other forms of life, for example, has now turned upon the scientist himself, reminding him that he, too, is an evolving being like any of those others. The observer himself is part of the observed; the scientist has been caught in his own scientific "net." Scientific knowledge, we have come to realize, is not the work of some omniscient spectator, who neither changes the reality he studies, nor is himself changed in the studying of it; knowledge of any sort is a kind of wedding between knowing subject and object known, resulting inevitably in the transformation of both parties. Instead of vainly trying to avoid stamping our human image on the realities we observe, we must acknowledge and assent to that stamping as an iron necessity of all knowledge.

Anthropocentrism, accordingly, and its inevitable result, some measure of anthropomorphism, simply cannot be banished from the activities of the scientist. Without giving rein to his subjectivity, the scientist could never practice science at all. But does this mean that no "objective" knowledge is attainable? Again, we recognize the specter Duhem had struggled to exorcise by his theory of science as "natural classification"; the question comes down with chilling bluntness to asking whether scientific knowledge has any "reality value" at all. It is a question of "saving science."

Teilhard's proposed solution remains essentially what it has always been. Suppose, just suppose, that there be one instance where the center of observation happens to coincide with the center of reality's own "construction." Typically, Teilhard proposes an illustration from geology—paleontology. Suppose one were trying to understand the way a certain portion of a mountain range came to take the shape it manifests to present-day observation. It might be that "chance"—or the workings of the educated geological eye—directs one's steps to a crossroads or to a point where valleys intersect. It can then happen that, all at once, the landscape "lights up"—the point of subjective observation happens to correspond perfectly with the point from which the "objective" landscape radiated outward in the historical process of its formation; the happy coincidence of these two points—visual and structural at once—might now permit the trained observer to "decode" the welter of clues which failed to make total sense until that moment of coincidence occurred.

Now, it may just happen,[8] Teilhard is persuaded, that humanity itself is just such a "point": the coincidence be-

---

[8] Teilhard uses a categorical form of the indicative at this point; my expository stance (he is anticipating on his total hypothesis) suggests this more conditional form of expression.

tween our necessary center of observation and the center of the world's evolutionary construction. If this be so, then anthropocentricism and anthropomorphism might become not only an unavoidable necessity to the scientific explorer, but a positive boon; the task of the scientist must then be defined as that of finding *how properly to exploit* that boon. *The Phenomenon of Man* invites the reader to assume, along with Teilhard, that in evolution's "natural history" humanity represents this coincidence of points, and to test that initial assumption by asking whether it permits us to achieve a "natural classification" of all evolving reality, from matter to mankind. If that effort succeeds, then the ring of truth which the mind hears when such a natural classification finally dawns upon it will serve as the guarantee that the subjective forms of thought we have applied were the correct ones, after all; we have asked reality a question in reality's own native language, not merely our own,[9] and the "naturalness" of the resulting classification gives us the assurance—the only necessary and sufficient assurance we have any right to ask—that reality itself has given *its* response.

It should be no surprise, Teilhard goes on to say, that it has taken humankind so long to learn the "language" of evolving reality. We are, after all, mere children in the evolutionary world which produced us: and we are still in the process of shedding the child's illusions that our world is small, that it has always been the same as now, and that it represents a welter of many disparate things with (apparently) little or no thread of unity bonding them into a single universe. To see our world as it genuinely is, our race has slowly learned that it must combat that triple illusion "of smallness, of plurality, of unchangingness."

---

[9] Since we humans are that evolving reality's own production, this correspondence should be no more difficult to accept than its corollary: that it required an evolution in our own way of "doing science" before nature's own language could become our reflective possession.

Those illusions, though, are not shared equally by our contemporaries. At this juncture we must remind ourselves of that other complication which makes *The Phenomenon of Man* a work requiring alertness of the reader: that Teilhard is compelled to address himself by turns to a variety of readers, variously aware of the universe science presents to us for our acceptance. Some of those readers are, of course, scientists, but even scientists are given to illusions which closer reflection on their activity as scientists—and on the history of science—should long since have banished. Others of his readers, he knew, would be proponents of so "spiritual" a view of humanity as to make them anti-scientific and, more specifically, anti-evolutionary in their sympathies.

Most scientists, for example, could be expected to possess and employ the "senses" which combat the unscientific mind's illusion of "smallness": the senses keyed to the "spatial immensity," temporal "depth," and bewildering "number" of the realities which greet the gaze of the scientifically educated eye. Most scientists, too, would have that sense of "proportion" which alerts them to the differences in "scale" separating infinitesimal atoms from vast nebulae. Those scientists especially concerned with the evolutionary aspects of our world would also have the sense of "movement" which combats the infantile illusion that the stars, continents, mountain ranges, animal species, and human races are now exactly what they always have been. But Teilhard will occasionally have to concern himself with educating the unscientific, or even anti-scientific, reader, to exercise those "senses" before they can appreciate even the problems he is about to deal with.[10]

---

[10] The meditation on the "Tree of Life" (PM 122–40/132–52) is a striking exercise designed to sharpen all these "senses." It occurs at a crucial juncture in the development of the "vision" which Teilhard is unfolding. Note that the very early essay on "The Face of the Earth" already anticipates the enumeration of the "senses" required to see the world which geology presents for our acceptance. See VP 44–45/65–67.

But there are scientists, he is equally convinced, whose sense of immensity and number is so well developed that they may have become blind to the physical and structural links in the "plurality" of our universe which oblige us to step back to view that plurality as a "whole," a constellation of "wholes," and, indeed, "organic" wholes.

That sense of sheer plurality is often enough connected with the scientist's blindness to "quality" and "novelty"; he may tend instinctively to think of reality as producing in its evolutionary process just so many different sorts of things, all on much the same level: all simply different "solutions" to the evolutionary problem of survival, but none of them in any genuine sense "superior" to their fellows. In scientists of this sort, Teilhard hopes, his work may awaken that sense of "quality" and "novelty" which permits them to see certain "absolute stages of perfection or growth"—to see that the cell is superior to the atom, the dog superior to the Venus's-flytrap, and a human being superior to every species of animal which preceded it in the vast evolutionary parade. This final sense of novelty, to which proponents of a "spiritual" view of mankind so often appeal—and rightly—the scientist would exercise now, but in a way less common among many spiritualistic thinkers: for while seeing humanity as a qualitative novelty, and a stage of evolutionary growth more perfect, absolutely, than its forerunners, he would succeed in doing so without eclipsing humanity's continuity with lower orders of evolutionary reality, hence "without upsetting the physical unity of the [evolving] world" to which a contemporary scientific view both is, and must be, legitimately loyal. That same sense, too, would complement the scientist's sense of "movement"; for instead of seeing reality's process as just so many periodic "monotonous repetitions" of occurrences producing the "same things" over and over again, this sense would alert the scientist to recognize the "entirely new," occasionally produced by the constantly rising "tide" concealed beneath those periodic "wave" movements.

Only when equipped with all these "senses," Teilhard contends, can we succeed in "placing" mankind scientifically; for up until now mankind has remained, for minds both scientific and anti-scientific, an "erratic object in a disjointed world"—an anomaly which betrays our inability to find, as yet, a satisfactory "natural classification" for the human group, a classification relating human individuals to humanity, humanity to the rest of life, and life itself as related to the natural history of the material universe.

What lines will that natural classification take? Historical lines, first of all. The natural history of our observable world must be seen as a history pivoting on three great "events": the birth of pre-living forms of matter, of life itself, and then, at humanity's advent, of "thought." The final phase of "anthropogenesis" must, accordingly, be viewed as climaxing the two successive phases of "cosmogenesis" which preceded, and prepared the way for, that final phase. In terms of present-day observation of our world, then, we must classify realities about us as respectively pertaining to one or other of the three "spheres," or terrestrial envelopes, to which these three events successively gave birth: lithosphere, biosphere, and noosphere. Not fancy neologisms, these, but classificatory tools, required by the task of "naturally" placing the human phenomenon as well as the rest of the reality whose evolutionary history produced that human phenomenon.

For humankind, Teilhard repeats, is truly a "phenomenon": not only in the more popular sense of being both "extraordinary and revealing," but more germanely here in the sense of representing a "genuine fact" as observable (for the most part) as any other "fact" to which scientists assent, and feel as scientists obliged to include within the

scope and methods of their efforts toward natural classification. This, moreover, is the meaning of that term "phenomenon" which gives Teilhard's entire essay its "special
character" as a "scientific *mémoire*" rather than a "metaphysical system." For Teilhard promises to restrict the evidence he adduces to what emerges from our "experience"
of man. But we must broaden that term "experience" to
include the entire array of "general" and "extended" acquaintance with humanity, gleaned from the sciences of
physics, biology, psychology, history, and sociology, as
well as from the indisputable evidence of our own consciousness of ourselves as self-reflective beings. We must,
among other things, leave off considering humankind as an
object of "scientific scrutiny" only as far as bodily characteristics are concerned—as most present-day science
tends to do. Even the most confirmed "positivist" can be
brought to see that humans are minds as well as matter,
and so can be persuaded to extend the range of significant
evidence to include these "interior" activities.

Yet we must not let that focus on interiority so high-
light the human being's "over-pronounced individuality"
as to blind us to the human "whole" to which each individual belongs, or so "break up nature into pieces" as to
blind ourselves to the "deep interrelations" and "measure-
less horizons" which link the human "whole" with the
whole of evolving life, and with that other whole, evolving
cosmic matter. This would be anthropocentrism in the
"bad" form which scientists quite rightly repudiate, but allow their repudiation of it to drive them to the opposite,
and equally unscientific, extreme.

Broaden the field of evidence this way, adopt the set of
senses required to banish our residual childish illusions
about humanity and reality more generally, reset all that
our experience tells us into the historical key, adjust our
classificatory tools to the dimensions of this new task, and
the result Teilhard promises is a vision of humanity, life,

and matter as a single continuous "unfolding whole," both "homogeneous" and "coherent": the "natural classification" of phenomena which science since before Aristotle has mutely striven to achieve. But nothing could be clearer: present-day science has failed to achieve that natural classification. The last thing Teilhard is claiming to "do" is present-day science; his hope is to present us with a preliminary sketch, no more than that, of the "true physics" which "one day" may be ours.

To "do" science in the currently accepted understanding of that term was, therefore, no part of the promise Teilhard made for his "scientific *mémoire*"; faulting him on that score simply proves that one cannot read very carefully. Accusing him of anthropocentrism and anthropomorphism is equally maladroit: he has gone to considerable lengths to show that even present-day science is irremediably victim to the very sins it has so persistently tried to avoid in its futile pursuit of that mythic posture, the pure "objectivity" of the omniscient spectator. All of this one could have extracted from an attentive and receptive reading of his Preface and Foreword: our study of his earlier essays serves merely to stimulate and illuminate such a reading of the terse and highly condensed observations he enclosed in those initial sections of *The Phenomenon of Man*.

It takes a fine blend of ignorance and arrogance to convict a man of not having done what he never claimed to do, and claimed, indeed, *not* to be doing in the first place. It takes a similar intellectual obtuseness to pounce upon him for having done, as though all innocent and unawares, what he has claimed the right to do. Teilhard is not doing "science" in the currently acceptable form of that genre; he could not have made that plainer. Trumpeting one's discovery of that fact is little more than breaking intellectual wind. But he is also being anthropocentric and anthropomorphic; he is being that of set purpose; he claims to have won his right to be so. To climb upon the parapets, as some of his critics have done, and triumphantly proclaim his anthropomorphism as though it were some dark and sinister secret he tried slyly to keep from his readers (he was, after all, a Jesuit, and you know those fellows) is an exercise in solemn silliness.

Those false issues cleared away, however, does Teilhard utterly abide all questions one might put to his manner of developing his personal vision of the past? Surely not yet. Before we are in a position to frame those questions correctly, though, we must have the patience to examine how that vision of the past is actually developed in *The Phenomenon of Man.*

10

Toward Evaluating
Teilhard's Vision
of the Past:
The Appropriate Questions

THE MOST CRUCIAL of Teilhard's working insights arose, we have seen, from his analysis of a particular anomaly bedeviling contemporary science; that anomaly was its failure, as he saw it, to fit the human phenomenon into anything resembling a satisfactory "natural classification." He could have *begun* his synthetic work, I have already suggested, where he began in his earlier essays, by focusing on that human phenomenon and highlighting the anomaly it represented. He could then have proposed the evidential and methodological readjustments ostensibly required to reduce that anomaly, and thus established the right to develop the film of cosmic events by running it backward in time, down through the tree of life to the origin of life from pre-living matter, in terms of those adjustments. This, we have seen, was his own order of discovery; it might (with hindsight) be reasonably argued that it would have furnished his readers with a more natural and convincing experience of discovery as well.

However one may judge his compositional strategy, the reader interested in recapturing his original discovery experience might well begin where he himself began, with his discussion of the human group in *The Phenomenon of Man*. The lines of that discussion are by now familiar: first, that the evolutionary birth of thinking beings constitutes a bothersome anomaly for the natural historian determined to classify humanity exclusively by consideration of his "outer" bodily characteristics (PM 163–64/179–80). The natural historian is not entirely misguided, however; for one thing, his deepest instinct as a scientist persuades him to respect humanity's evolutionary "continuity" with the primates and lower orders of vertebrates, indeed, with the entire historic stream of life, pre-life, and evolving cosmic matter from which humanity emerged. The privileged locus for proving that evolution did in fact occur is what it always was, both for Teilhard and his fellow-naturalists; the series of family resemblances among the vertebrates, traced backward in time, from fully developed fossil back to earlier preliminary "sketches," can scarcely be understood in other than evolutionary terms (PM 130–31, 122–30/ 140–42, 132–40). Tracing that process forward in time, on the other hand, the naturalist is compelled by the evidence to envisage it somewhat on the model of a "tree," its limbs and branches ramifying outward in the organized way which our minds instinctively recognize as the "natural" result of a "growth" process (PM 137–40/148–52). Evolution did occur, therefore—the fact of that is clear beyond doubting, despite the numerous disagreements which persist among scientists on "how" the process must have worked. Examine the fossil evidence of early man's original forms (PM 184–90/203–10), and it is abundantly clear that man, somatically at least, is continuous with the primate ancestors from which the human group has sprung.

But the almost negligible differences in somatic characteristics between man and prehuman primates give us no clue to why humanity should, in so short a span of geological time, have spread like a brush fire across the round earth, subduing all competing forms of life before it, and in a cosmic instant, as it were, have radically transformed the face of our entire planet (PM 191–212/211–235). This immense biological importance of the human group —evident on the purely phenomenological level, be it noted—is totally disproportionate with those nearly infinitesimal somatic differences; hence, the nagging anomaly which the appearance and spread of mankind represents for contemporary systems of scientific "classification" (PM 163–64/179–80).

How to account for this amazing phenomenon of spread, conquest, and planetary transformation whereby humanity enclosed the earth like a new "envelope"? The answer is obvious: the fossil evidence puts it beyond any question that man's capacity for "invention" and social organization was responsible. But these are not somatic properties; they clearly emerge from the "psychic" transformation from which humanity stood forth as the only form of life capable of self-reflection. That process must be thought of as recasting at a stroke all the cosmic materials humanity inherited from the earth and tree of life which gave it birth: a process whereby the once pre-living matter of our planet has itself been "hominized." But it must also be thought of in fresh categories: as a continuously prepared leap into discontinuity, the crossing of a "critical threshold." And the new planetary "envelope" resulting from matter's hominization must be thought of in fresh categories as well— not simply as a "family" or "subgroup" of the primates, but as a radically new "sphere" into which evolving matter has "broken": a thought sphere, or "noosphere."

But it will not do, Teilhard is aware, to propose an entirely new set of categories and classificatory schemata for the sole purpose of dealing with the human phenomenon. That would amount to merely sewing new patches on the garment of an older classificatory system, an *ad hoc* procedure which would run directly counter to the evidence of humanity's continuity with earlier forms of life and matter, and put the desired "natural classification" of humanity beyond all scientific reach. To be acceptable, scientifically, those categories and classificatory tools must be shown to apply to the entirety of the evolutionary process, and to each of its three grand phases. Invention, socialization, critical thresholds, spheres or planetary envelopes—all these must apply to, and indeed positively illumine, the scientist's legitimate effort to put some order into the process from beginning to end. Not only that, but all that was valid in the older classificatory system must be accounted for, and subsumed without distortion into any newer classification which would lay claim to greater "naturalness"; in other terms, the "ways" or "laws" of evolutionary process discovered on prehuman levels must be shown, *ceteris paribus*, on the human level as well.

Responding to this challenge, Teilhard invites us to focus on the "history" of the human group; it is the group best known to us, when all is said. Hypothesize for a moment that examining the history of that group will provide us with the "key" to a clearer vision of how evolution operates than even the history of the vertebrates formerly did. The result, he proposes, is nothing less than an "illumination."

Illuminated, first of all, is the law of "structure" which evolution obeys on every level of its operation, from matter to humanity. Clear the eye of the hard and fast distinction between "natural" and "artificial," and the human group in its process of multiplication shows up as "fanning out" or "branching" into verticils, all different from each other. But those differences are complementary, with the complementarity which betrays interdependence. Despite their plurality (or because of it), both individuals and groups, observed at sufficient distance, show up as bonded into a single organic unity; not merely a collection, humanity appears to the educated eye as quite literally an "organism."

Not only the structure, but the "mechanism" of evolutionary advance, is clearer when discovered in the human group; for humanity advances by a series of "groping" efforts which from time to time blossom forth into "inventions"—of tools, techniques, social forms, what have you. It may seem at first that groping and invention must be the exclusive property of this self-reflective group; but take the hint, explore afresh the lower levels, and see whether analogous, not merely metaphorical, anticipations of it show up once we know what to look *for*.

And while exploring those lower levels, look for confirmation of what the human group additionally suggests about the law of "movement" presiding over the entire evolutionary process: that it may represent, beneath all those seemingly random and self-repeating waves, the mounting of a single psychic "tide," the rise and expansion of matter to consciousness, of consciousness to self-reflective thought.

This, then, is the full arsenal of conceptual tools which Teilhard invites his fellow-scientists, and non-scientists as well, to apply to each of the three major phases of the evolutionary process: to apply them, and by applying to test their serviceability. But he asks us to bear in mind that what is being tested is a total theory; it is, in the last event, that total theory which must be compared with the "facts" as we know them in order to see whether it succeeds in offering our minds a "natural classification" of those facts. But, Teilhard was persuaded, he had won the right to see those "facts" in a novel way: as the "imposed factors" in the natural history of the evolving real, which science in its procession of theories "translates" into "scientific facts."

It is not my intention to present here a "reading" of *The Phenomenon of Man* in its entirety: that would require a book in itself. But to clarify Teilhard's procedure in its actual operation, let me take his initial section on pre-living matter as an illustration (PM 39–66/33–48).

We are, first of all, dealing here mainly with the findings of physics and of chemistry, both inorganic and organic.

But Teilhard's hypothesis compels him to take those findings as reflecting the "history" of pre-living matter, and to search for the "imposed factors" which pre-living matter must have exhibited. First of all, Teilhard proposes, that original matter must have been characterized by plurality, but a plurality bonded into unity, and a unified plurality of elements each of which is a reservoir of energy. The original plurality must be seen, then, as a "system," a unified "totum" or "whole," containing a fixed quantum of energy.

But the original plurality can be further characterized; each element would appear to have borne a certain family resemblance to every other: they were all made up of nuclei and electrons, and, further, they were all engaged in a mysterious process of complexification which seems to have begun in the "laboratories" we know as stars. Mendeleeff's classic table of the elements, from simplest to more and more complex, becomes in this perspective a biography of pre-living matter as it passed through these various stages of complexification.

But, it might be objected, these characterizations of "original matter" are so minimal and general that they tell us very little. To this Teilhard replies that their minimal character is the best guarantee of the confidence we may have that no future physics will prove us wrong in accepting them. Besides, notice that we are compelled, in trying to characterize the original pre-living matter which went into later evolutionary syntheses, to work from what contemporary physics theorizes about the properties and behavior of the present-day matter which comes under its contemporary observations; we cannot avoid them entirely, but we must at least minimize the risks involved in extrapolating into the past too much detail of what we know about matter at this advanced stage in cosmic evolution.

But minimal though these "imposed factors" may seem,

they are enough for our purposes. For once original matter has been identified as energetic rather than inert, and as engaged in that process of complexification, we are in a position to confront the anomaly resulting from the way purely "quantitative" and mathematical physics deals with complexification: the anomaly of entropy. That anomaly entitles Teilhard to mount his argument for generalizing that "aberrant phenomenon," the "within," and then to proceed to propose (as "imposed factors" once again) the more "qualitative" laws of complexification which suggest themselves once a certain measure of "within"—extremely granular on simpler levels, but becoming more powerful and influential on levels of greater complexity—has been accepted as an "imposed factor property" of original pre-living matter. Immediately the picture jumps out of one focus into another. The complexification phenomenon has been reset into a more "biological" key; we are prompted to "see" original matter, instead of as engaged in a downward entropic drift, as already "thrusting" energetically toward the greater complexity which will afford it larger and larger measures of both consciousness and spontaneity. Evolution has already begun, has already manifested in rudimentary ways how it will operate throughout the future, has already declared itself as the dominant, primordial, and therefore scientifically more significant, current traversing the entirety of the material universe. The "scientific facts" of contemporary physical theory have been respected, but when illuminated from a different angle, have simply changed in meaning. Instead of vindicating its claim to be the fundamental behavior pattern of pre-living matter, entropic drift has been relegated to a secondary role; it represents the vast but inevitable evolutionary "wastage" this total theory would lead us to expect—vast, inevitable, and quantitatively more impressive than the upward thrusting spiral, but precisely because "within," at this stage, is so granular and minimal in power.

Teilhard has alerted his readers to the linkage which his theory establishes between those two major anomalies of present-day science: to set up his argument for the generalized presence of "within," he took the right to anticipate what the existence of the human phenomenon suggests, so that the anomaly of humanity's place in evolving nature casts its light before, illumining the anomalous opposition between entropic drift and the upward spiral of life. Now, with these conceptual tools in place, he has won the right to probe for the "imposed factors" which show the complexification process in the materials of our early earth as already "branching" into the less productive crystallizing world and the more productive world of "polymers" (PM 67–74/65–73).[1] Though they represent, quantitatively, a minority when compared with those elements which "chose" the lower road of crystallization, he argues that the polymers of organic chemistry represent, qualitatively, the more significant population. They declared their ancient presence even before life came, and spread over the closed volume of our planet to constitute a new "envelope" or "sphere" which must be seen as a "whole": a critical threshold has been crossed with the formation of this polymer sphere. But the closed volume represented by the round earth must be expected to induce, over countless ages, an increase in "tension" or "pressure" in that polymer sphere; the power of "within," like the waters of a closed kettle brought gradually to a boil and turning into steam, must be expected to undergo a "change of state": thrusting in its nearly blind "groping" way for ever-more-productive modes of outer complexification, matter fails billions of times (as one would expect), but then, at long last, "invents" that array of ingenious solutions to the problem, the world of mega-molecules. That sublife world permits

---

[1] Teilhard makes the reader aware that, authorized by his method of detecting "imposed factors," he is using this term in a wider connotation than the conventional chemical sense; see PM 70n1/69n1.

"within" an even greater range of (still vastly reduced) consciousness, spontaneity, and groping inventiveness; again the pressure builds, a change of state occurs, and matter crosses the critical threshold into "cellularity": evolution has succeeded in producing life.

Again, what Teilhard has done is this: he has examined what the sciences of inorganic and organic chemistry reveal about the matter of our present world, matter which is found in various stages, and in different types, of complex arrangements; he has translated that information into the language of imposed factors, then situated each stage as a "phase" or chapter in our planet's natural history. Then he has taken the right already won to "see" these various chapters from "within"—as pre-living matter's groping process toward inventing life. None of the original scientific information, he would argue, has been distorted; it has merely been translated into the language of his total theory.

But how are we to judge the fidelity of that "translation"? By awaiting the complete unfolding of the theory itself, the whole of it being contained and presupposed in any single one of its parts, and then asking whether it commends itself to our minds as a natural–historical classification of everything observation tells us about our world. The anthropomorphic terms "groping," "ingenuity," "thrust," and "invention" may initially seem alien, even disconcerting to our minds—particularly if we fail to make the "correction for analogy" on which Teilhard repeatedly insists; but if such terms are truly appropriate to evolution on the human scale, they cannot be entirely and absolutely inappropriate for describing the ways of evolution on all, even its lowest, and earliest, levels.

There are a number of assumptions implied in Teilhard's very way of framing the problem to his readers. One could, conceivably, pose questions or objections to any or all of them. He assumes, first off, that we share with him the conviction that science, avowedly or no, does in its development aim at the construction of such a single, unitary, total theory of the observable real, and legitimately so; secondly, that we are convinced that any such theory, to fit the evolving world, must take the form of a single "natural history"; thirdly, that we are informed enough to understand why the problem of the scientific "knowledge" of reality is, indeed, a very real problem; fourthly, that we are informed, and also concerned enough about (and even convinced of), the "reality value" of scientific knowledge, and able intelligently to follow and assent to his argument that such reality value can be guaranteed any scientific theory if and only if it presents the mind with a satisfying "natural classification" of the realities it takes into its explanatory purview; and, finally, that we agree with him that the twin properties of coherence and homogeneity must characterize the logical development of any satisfactory theory in order to persuade the mind that its logical connections correspond to the true ontological contours of the phenomenal real. The "same" conceptual tools must prove serviceable throughout, the "same" laws and structures verified at every level, and if it be a single natural "history," it must (ideally) map certain laws of "recurrence" operating at each of the various stages of a single "movement."

If we fully understand and agree with each of these propositions, Teilhard is confident, we must then agree with him that "science" at this point of its own evolutionary development furnishes us with no such total theory. The most glaring evidence of that is the division of science into a variety of sciences, all operating with disparate methods, canons of evidence, and priorities. The most crucial rupture in this skein of sciences occurs at the moment science is called upon to classify humanity as a scientific phenomenon; man represents the most disconcerting of the various anomalies science has not yet found a way to deal with. Another anomaly, however, occurs at the moment when science is invited to relate the evolutionary ascent of life to the downward entropic drift of non-living matter. But a whole subset of anomalies flows from these two major ones: that the sciences of matter deal primarily with analyzing the behavior of large numbers, and treat that behavior as the result of an amalgam of chance and determinism, in which individual elements are envisaged primarily (if not exclusively) as passively reacting to pressures and impacts coming from "without"; whereas psychology, history, sociology—in short, the sciences of man—must take primary account of individual persons, regarding them as consciously, spontaneously, and even freely active "interiorities." This is the interiority which—another anomaly, if you like—spiritualistic thinkers are not entirely wrong in pointing to as evidence that humans do, and always will, elude classification in scientific terms.

Now, Teilhard is convinced that if we consent to the aspiration toward a total scientific theory, and to the requirements laid down for its realization; if, further, we assent to these various anomalies as precisely that; then we will be receptive to the need for new scientific thought-instruments designed to reduce, even eliminate, these anomalies, succeed in classifying humanity more "naturally" than now, and correlate entropic drift with life's ascent as the two "faces" we should expect of one single "movement," once that movement has been properly understood. That theory we shall find all the more satisfying to our minds, and *eo ipso* bringing a more "natural" order out of the evidence we are dealing with, if those various sub-anomalies can also be eliminated, individual vs. mass effects, passivity vs. activity, determinism vs. freedom, and others like them.

Now, it might be objected, with some justice, that none of these Teilhardian affirmations about science is a strictly "scientific" affirmation; that they pertain, on the contrary, to the discipline which today fits under the rubric of "philosophy of science." True enough. But Pierre Duhem was, after all, pleased to call himself a "physicist" even when writing his philosophy of physics; and though Teilhard may have been a trifle sanguine in thinking that scientists could be counted on to have pondered these matters all that seriously, he had little need to feel that such considerations were out of place in a *mémoire* which claimed to be "scientific" in the Jeansian meaning of the genre.

The same "scientific" pedigree, he implicitly claimed, attached to the different adjustments which he urged scientists to make in order to elaborate successfully the single total theory to which they aspire.

For some of those adjustments are hardly new; they already represented in his own time current scientific procedure—scientific, that is, in the eyes of certain of the sciences, at least. For example, he asks us, not to suspend analytic procedures entirely, merely to complement those procedures with the more synthetic, middle- and long-distance visions of things as "wholes"—as the comparative anatomist already does, and finds indispensable. From seeing wholes to envisaging the evolutionary process in terms of three major "spheres" is but a step: one which the geologist Suess had already partially suggested in his work on continent formation. He would have us recognize that "consciousness" and "interiority" are phenomena as "real" for science as mass or velocity: but this is something historians, psychologists, and sociologists already do.

But assume such consciousness and interiority on levels of pre-human life, and, indeed, in some sense even on pre-living levels: this is one of Teilhard's proposals which send shock waves through the conventional scientific community. And yet, it shouldn't. The scientist's choices are two and only two. Either silently ignore such "interior" properties, dismissing them as mere "aberrancies"; or resolutely take the opposite tack, the one which the history of scientific progress argues is the only scientifically profitable one: accept the troubling phenomenon as the phenomenon it is, and probe for its "generalized" presence and meaning from top to bottom of the evolutionary scale. So science was compelled to do with the phenomenon of radiation; so too we are compelled to recognize that the variation of mass with velocity holds for *all* velocities, though originally *uncovered* only where such velocities approach the speed of light. This familiar strategy of generalizing what initially appeared to be an "aberrant" phenomenon implies that radiation and mass-velocity variation occur not simply with radium, or at extremely high velocities, but everywhere in the world of matter, even where they are so much less noticeable as to be virtually undetectable. What truly *scientific* reason can there be for refusing to apply a similar "generalization" to consciousness and interiority, and to their companion properties, ingenuity, invention, spontaneity, conspiration, and socialization? Indeed, the only reason one can adduce for such an exclusion comes down to a mechanistic prejudice; but that, a moment's reflection will show, is precisely the kind of "metaphysical" assumption which the scientist owes it to the autonomy of science sedulously to avoid. Now, one is tempted to ask, who is being truly scientific: Jacques Monod or Teilhard de Chardin?[2]

[2] Monod asserts that, contrary to the view he admits many biologists would prefer, living beings must be considered as "teleonomic" (*Chance and Necessity*, pp. 8–9), but a few sentences further on, speaks nonetheless of such beings as "machines" (pp. 10–13). This may be consistent with the thesis which he means to prove: that even such teleonomy can ultimately be understood, scientifically, in mechanistic terms (see esp. p. 40, but also pp. 23–44, 59–61, 79–80). Monod's unalterable epistemological axiom governing all such scientific explanation is, however, the principle of scientific "objectivity," which he (somewhat arbitrarily) interprets as outlawing all explanatory appeal to "aims" or "purposes" (pp. 20–22). The implicit recognition that aims and purposes both operate, and indeed are "chosen," on the human level (pp. 173–79) seems partially to account for the "flagrant epistemogical contradiction" he first proclaims (pp. 20–22) and subsequently is obliged to eliminate from his own effort to explain even human activity "objectively" as the blind product of chance and necessity (pp. xi–xiv, 3–4, 9, 14, 20–22, 24, 138–80). Hence,

But that "generalization" process must not be imagined in some crude and silly way; interiority does not take the same form or exert the same power in the tree as in the dog, or in the dog as in the self-reflective human being. But the scientist is scarcely unfamiliar with the legitimacy and illuminating power of such analogies; without that familiarity he could not, for example, even deal skillfully with that omnipresent tool of his trade, the scientific "model." Aristotle experiences "energy" in the human arm which lifts a weight, but is hardly fooled when he applies the term—analogously—to a lightning flash and a racehorse. The trick is, not to avoid analogy, but to know how to use it properly; to recognize that when we speak of "interiority" in an atom, cell, plant, orangutan, and human being, we are saying the "same" thing of all of them, but the "sameness" is at once shot through with differences, sometimes so immense that we can only very indirectly imagine what the dog's interiority must be like, much less that of the plant, or cell, or molecule.

But that principle of analogy will apply not only to properties, but to processes and laws as well. Socialization in the atoms of a molecule, the ants of a hill, and the humans gathered around some prehistoric fire is in some sense the "same," but in others a vastly different process. Tension can build between the poles of approaching magnets as

---

Monod seems, on the one hand, to accept (with Duhem and Teilhard) the legitimacy of the aspiration toward a unitary science of the real, while, on the other, fudging on the predictability normally associated with such deterministic explanations (see the pages referred to above, along with pp. 42–44).

But accept the breach between the "objective" sciences of matter and the indispensably "subjective" interpretations of human activity, and the aspiration toward a unitary science immediately calls into question Monod's version of the principle of "objectivity" as precisely that which stands in the way of achieving that unitary science. That question promptly turns into one directed against the mechanistic assumptions to which Monod tranquilly holds; Teilhard and Duhem both argue that mechanism is, after all, not a scientific, but a metaphysical, theory. Nowhere do I see Monod even confronting the case they make for that claim, though it lies at the heart of the issues dividing him and Teilhard.

well as between competing human cultures; the laws governing the results of such tension-rises must, if reality be continuous, be in some real sense the "same," even though operating in vastly different ways, particularly when a "critical threshold" separates-while-joining the realms in which those laws are operative.

With that conceptual tool, the "critical threshold," we come to a second class of readjustments Teilhard invites his fellow-scientists to make, with keen awareness that they may find them "new" and less familiar. The scientist, especially when limiting his observations to the observable "exterior" of things, is given to stress the continuities between, for example, anthropoids and primitive humans. The notion of a "threshold" combining *both* continuity and discontinuity may strike such a scientist as paradoxical, even queer to the extent of being contradictory and therefore unacceptable.[3] And yet, Teilhard points out, the notion should not be all that strange to him: geometry makes use of it in describing the properties of a cone, and the "boiling point" when a liquid changes state and becomes a gas is just another common example of a critical threshold. Such paradoxical notions may be *more* familiar to philosophers of nature and metaphysicians striving to understand the mysterious reality of "change"; but such paradoxes are not by any means philosophers' exclusive property, and the scientist after a little reflection should be able to deal with them as comfortably as he succeeded in becoming comfortable with complementary theories of light or the apparent paradoxes in relativity theory.

Applying the notion of critical threshold, however, requires the acceptance of Teilhard's proposed "law" of complexity consciousness, or of something very like that law.

[3] If, that is, the scientist grasps both sides of the paradox in the first place. Witness the number of critics who have attacked Teilhard for making the human reductively "continuous" with the subhuman, with no acknowledgement of the discontinuity simultaneously implied in the notion of critical threshold.

Every scientist is familiar with the phenomenon of increased complexity, and more than one has pointed out its troubling implications for probability thinking. That anti-probabilistic trend exhibited in the ascent of life forms has suggested the operation of a mysterious "anti-chance" factor in the evolutionary process, a resurgence of Lamarckian thinking which the more scientifically orthodox Darwinian understandably resents. But from the moment that "within," or some measure of interiority, is admitted as operative on every level of material reality, not only has a new name been given this anti-chance factor, but a new problem arises: how to correlate the operations of interiority with the observable increase in outer complexity?

The conceptual step one takes in hypothesizing that increased complexity correlates somehow with an increase in interiority's power is scarcely a giant step; in fact, it is almost a banality. That correlation, Teilhard reminds us (if we need reminding), is far from simple, and we cannot in the present state of our knowledge claim to have its formula. But the very slipperiness of that correlation allows for two definite and associated possibilities: (*a*) that there may be moments in evolutionary history where a giant stride in within-power can occur in association with an apparently negligible rearrangement in complexity; and (*b*) that some sort or sorts of complexification may be more crucial than others, more crucial because more capable of vehicling such strides in interiority.

It was not Teilhard's discovery that nervous systems and brains were just such a crucial sort of complexification; common to paleontologists who had for decades measured the brain-pans of their fossils, that notion was almost trite. Teilhard's suggestion is that we apply this parameter, crucial to the study of our primitive *human* ancestors, to the *entire range* of evolving life-forms; indeed, that we reduce every other morphological family-relationship among our fossil specimens to a secondary place, and firmly focus on this parameter in hopes it will arrange our specimens at last into a "natural" classification. Not the *discovery* of braininess,[4] but the resolute choice of it as the open-sesame of a total natural classification of evolving reality, this precisely is his proposal: whether we are exploring human finds, or lemurs, or even insects, he tells us to "look at heads" to allow the plot of the evolutionary film to disengage itself from its numerous sub-plots and digressions, and leap into focus for our eyes.

But choosing brains and nervous systems as the "Ariadne's thread" through evolution's labyrinth implies that we are also prepared to accept the corollary of that choice: the "psychic" character of evolution. The implications of that acceptance are, in turn, twofold, at least: it implies, first of all, that we are ready to regard every instance of cephalic morphological complexification as an evolutionary thrust toward higher forms of psychic functioning; but it also means, secondly, that we are prepared to turn our usual order of thinking on its head, and to see all morphological changes as emanating from this psychic current flowing through the entire process. Just as the human warrior's temperament and soul prompts him to invent the tools of battle, so, in some obscure way and in reduced measure, the predator soul of the tiger lay behind, and expressed itself in, the evolution of its saber teeth. As always, the trick consists in applying, analogously, a "law" discoverable on evolution's human level to all the antecedent levels which eventually produced the human.

The warrior example, however, brings up another conceptual readjustment Teilhard is asking us boldly to make. For to "see" the evolutionary character of human history, we must accept the "artificial" inventions of the warrior as "natural" and "biological" in nature and import, as "natural" and "biological" as the tiger's saber tooth. A somewhat

---

[4] As Medawar mockingly implies on pp. 101–103 of his review, cited in the Introduction, note 2, above.

shocking readjustment, this, especially to thought ways deeply rutted by convention: but then, is there anything so radically implausible in it? And hasn't the progress of science depended at critical moments on such initially shocking readjustments? And isn't the test of all such readjustments, finally, whether they furnish us with a classification of reality *more* natural than the one which went before it?

One could, I repeat, pose questions or objections to any and all of the assumptions Teilhard supposes his readers will share with him about the ideal unity of science and the conditions for the realization of that ideal; about the reality and location of the anomalies which frustrate, for now, that aspiration; about the value and legitimacy of the conceptual readjustments he proposes in order to reduce those anomalies by transforming them into positive illuminants for a science which he claims, once having accepted them, will not only remain scientific, but become even more genuinely "scientific" than at present. But, these, I submit, represent the first phalanx of questions which are truly appropriate and even mandatory for anyone interested in making a serious evaluation of *The Phenomenon of Man* and the "vision of the past" encased in it.[5]

Once those more foundational issues have been dealt with, a second phalanx of questions commands attention. These are closer to the kinds of questions critics like Medawar and Simpson put, but with an impatient haste which prevented them from seeing *how* they must be framed in order to qualify as valid questions to Teilhard's synthesis. In baldest terms, then, do the "scientific facts" support, in the last analysis, the total hypothesis and cluster of subhypotheses Teilhard invites us to entertain? The question needs reframing, but the preoccupation which prompts it is, at least, a valid one. For the "coherence and homogenei-

---

[5] I must remind the reader one final time of the limited focus of this study, and the limited claims I make in consequence.

ty" Teilhard repeatedly trumpets as the twin marks of a "natural" classification must not be considered merely "logical" properties of a theory our minds find satisfying. The theory was always meant to "arrange" the facts as observation reveals them to the educated eye; indeed, it must boast that further property, heuristic "fertility," whereby its proposals suggest further reaches for subsequent observation.

But to be a valid question posed to the total theory encased in *The Phenomenon of Man*, that question about "scientific facts" either need not be asked at all, or if asked, needs reframing. It need not be asked at all if one refuses to accept the ideal of science and the readjustments to present scientific practice which we have been considering up to now; but once one accepts them, or is simply willing to entertain them as plausible to see where the argument leads from there, the question needs reframing. For it is simply illegitimate to complain that a radically readjusted scientific theory derives no support from, or even runs counter to, what passed for "facts" in a preceding theory which needed that radical readjustment.

Consider once again the lesson to be drawn from the continuous progress in scientific theories: if the discovery of evolution tells us anything, it tells us that science itself is still in swaddling clothes, and that we would be ill-advised to hitch our conceptual wagons too firmly to this or that contemporary scientific theory, taking it as the latest and therefore absolutely final word which science has to tell us about reality. Nor must that procession of scientific theories tempt us into a nihilistic skepticism toward science. The safest and sanest course is to explore each level of the real *through* the lens of scientific theories, searching for the "imposed factors" which the observable real must possess in order to understand the very succession of theories, each one surpassing its predecessors in precision, but surpassing them by subsuming and completing all that made them "true" for their lifetime. The only *appropriate* question to Teilhard's synthesis is, accordingly, whether it succeeds in properly identifying those "imposed factors" of the real, and in classifying them "naturally."

Should we, for example, opt uniquely for Neo-Darwinian over competing Neo-Lamarckian modes of explaining the workings of evolution? That way we would, at least, be opting for "the latest" in present-day science. But that exclusive choice, Teilhard implicitly warns in *The Phenomenon of Man*, however stylish in the estimate of contemporary biologists, might well turn out to be as short-lived in its usefulness as it might be short-sighted in the light of science's brief history. Every theory which science has been forced to discard was "the latest" up to the date of its being discarded. And in this particular case, the "facts" (in another, valid sense of the expression) argue against such exclusivity. There are too many phenomena observable on evolution's human level—ingenuity and invention, the acquisition and inheritance of culture, religion, learning, and social forms of every sort—which only Neo-Lamarckian forms of thought can take account of and "explain" as a total scientific theory must explain them. But, it must also be admitted, even on that human level, Neo-Darwinian thought forms do not lose all appropriateness: for in the history of mankind we meet with all sorts of inertial passivity, the play of large numbers, the importance of somatic characteristics and genetic inheritance. Again, the trick which Teilhard would have us manage is to view the entire evolutionary process *through* the suggestive lenses furnished by these competing, and quite possibly complementary, theories, in hopes that eventually a further theory may emerge subsuming the "truth" in both of them. Neo-Lamarckianism seems "truer" when applied to the human level, and Neo-Darwinism truer on lower levels of evolution. But for the moment, once the continuity of the human group with all its evolutionary forebears is granted, we must look for ever-more-distant analogies of the Neo-Lamarckian characteristics, so evident in human evolutionary history, at all other stages in evolution's workings; and we must be alert, as well, to Neo-Darwinian factors, more dominant in earlier stages of that process, but present and still active on the human level.

In summary, Teilhard is far from recommending that we accept at face value all the "latest" that science claims to tell us about the real; science is too young for that,[6] and too many dissonances remain, among the various sciences as well as between science and our more extended acquaintance with the real. What we must do, therefore, is bear in mind not only the claims of science but those persistent dissonances as well, then probe for the "imposed factors" which must lie behind both scientific models and those residual dissonances. Only then have we a grounded hope of constructing the total "scientific" theory, the natural history of our world, to which science unavoidably, and irresistibly, aspires.

This is not poetry, though poets might love it; not metaphysics, though metaphysicians might find it nourishing for their speculations. It is not theology or religion, though theologians and religious believers may find it quite congenial. Nor is it mysticism, though when writing in that entirely different genre, Teilhard could hold his own. It would be more exact to see its foundational elements as emerging from a "philosophy of science," one which any more than

[6] Monod bases his loyalty to the principles of "objectivity" (see note 2 above) on the fact that science has clung to it for the past three hundred years. Even conceding the figure for the sake of argument (and ignoring the possibility that history, sociology, and psychology may lay claim to being "sciences"), one wonders: are three centuries, in the history of ideas, such an awesomely long time? A glance through Alfred North Whitehead's *Adventures of Ideas* raises some salutary questions about any such estimate.

routine scientist, reflecting on the practice and history of his *métier*, could accept. But the foundations once assured, the vision of the past presented in the first three sections of *The Phenomenon of Man* is neither more nor less than what Teilhard claimed for it: a total "scientific" theory, in which the term science has taken on a new, but also a very ancient, meaning—the meaning it had when Aristotle wrote his *Physics*.

Afterword

NO ONE CAN EVER WRITE A BOOK and then confidently predict how what he has written will eventually be read. That gap between the written and the read got to bedevil Duhem and, after him, Teilhard. To a lesser, but still serious, degree, it seems that the same gap has inserted itself between my very first reader and me.

I had asked Fordham University Press to choose, as the "outside reader" they wisely insist upon for all their publications, someone more abreast of recent developments in the philosophy of science than I could claim to be. This they did. Their choice was a good one as far as I was concerned; his reading of my exposé was careful and sympathetic, and his evaluation kindly enough that I wish here to express my thanks to him, anonymous though he will remain.

He did, though, conclude his remarks with three sets of critical comments. Fordham University Press extended the courtesy of allowing me (for which, more thanks) to see and reply to them before the members of their editorial board came to their decision about publishing this work. The dialogue of comment and reply the members of the editorial board found illuminative enough that they requested that I incorporate some of its results in the finished text. I am happy to comply with this suggestion. Hence, this Afterword.

"Some," Reader suggested, "will be disappointed . . . mostly by what is, or may appear to be, left out" of the foregoing pages; and notably, by the fact that this book "does not take its cue from, or refer to, recent literature of a genre similar to Teilhard's work. . . ." He goes on, in his second point, to specify what "genre" he had in mind:

"Teilhard's work on evolution and Christianity is now paralleled by a rash of works attempting to do similar things with quantum physics, cosmology, etc., and other religious traditions, e.g., [Fritjof] Capra's *Tao of Physics*[1] and [Gary] Zukav's *The Dancing Wu Li Masters. . . .*"[2] This "new literary genre . . . dealing with the religious meaning of scientific theories" uses "strategies" which are "comparable with those Teilhard used," and "some readers might want to know how such a genre is to be defined and evaluated" and how Teilhard's work is "situated" in relation to it.

Here, I submit, my critic has fallen into a classic trap of the book reviewer: he is regretting the fact that I did not write *another* book than this, one on Teilhard's *religious* thought, a book which he himself might be more interested in reading, or perhaps even writing. But I chose to write this book; I even had some qualms about too tiresomely bludgeoning my readers on the deliberately limited point this book was written to drive home: the precise sense in which, and the grounds on which, Teilhard claimed that the "vision of the past" encased in the first three sections of *The Phenomenon of Man* could legitimately be called "scientific."[3] That claim has been derided, flatly called into question, or, by some friendlier critics, cheerfully explained away in damning accents of praise for Teilhard's poetic, religious, metaphysical, or mystical powers. The Teilhard emerging from this barrage of appreciation sported a number of caps: scientist, poet, theologian, visionary. But blazoned on each of those caps was the label "brilliant amateur," with the all-too-frequent undertone "not *really*

---

[1] *The Tao of Physics: An Exploration of the Parallels Between Modern Physics and Eastern Mysticism* (Berkeley: Shambala, 1975).

[2] *The Dancing Wu Li Masters: An Overview of the New Physics* (New York: Morrow, 1979).

[3] See above, Introduction, pp. 5–6; chap. 9, p. 135; chap. 10, p. 170; chap. 4, note 2; chap. 10, note 5. All these reminders of my limited intention in these pages remain exactly as they stood in the copy Reader examined.

to be taken seriously." It would be attempting too much, in a single study, to relabel all those caps: my single-minded preoccupation here has been to relabel one of them, and only one, to "thorough professional."

This does, I admit, have something to do with Teilhard's religious thought, eventually at least. For he himself was deadly serious in making the "scientific" claims he made, and his reasons for that were of the soundest: any proposal dealing with the "religious meaning of scientific theories" like that of evolution must, especially when coming from a Christian, touch bedrock through its contact with and respect for the real as humans best know it to be.[4] My critic is asking me to unfold what I have repeatedly termed the "larger dialectic" which went into Teilhard's synthesis of Christianity and evolution; others, notably Madeleine Barthélémy-Madaule, have capably dealt with that elsewhere. But Teilhard was keenly aware that he must first lay the foundations for that larger dialectic by a prior (and more limited) dialectic which defended science's view that our world did in fact evolve, and evolved in such a way as fundamentally coheres with the Christian view of that very same world; otherwise, his subsequent efforts at theological synthesis would amount to so many dream-castles, floating in imagination's cloud-cuckoo-land. No one, to my knowledge, had carefully explored that prior set of claims; it seemed to me a job worth taking on, and once taken on, quite job enough for one book. That, and no other book, is the one I have chosen to write; understandably, I think, that choice entailed not responding to every conceivable question which every imaginable reader might have about everything Teilhard had to say.

---

[4] The historical and "incarnational" character of Christianity, to which Teilhard was constantly sensitive, obliges him to respect the resistant particularity of "the facts" perhaps more scrupulously than a Taoist or Buddhist might feel obliged to do. Hence, the connection he strives to establish (in his "larger" dialectic) among evolutionary theory, the "natural history" of the universe, and Christianity as the "historical axis" of human evolution.

elimination as it were, the entire array of currently accepted conventional sciences?

It would be comforting to have a clearer answer to that question, but I confess to knowing no peremptory passages in which Teilhard squarely confronts this issue, once it is put this precisely. The best I have been able to uncover is a series of suggestive remarks which lead one to believe, or at least to suspect, this much: (*a*) that it did not overly concern Teilhard to speculate about, much less predict, whatever kinds of transformation might affect the conventional sciences; (*b*) that there might always remain a gap between the entire array of conventional sciences and the novel type of science he proposed in order to attain to a more unitary, coherent, and "true" vision of the evolutionary past; and (*c*) that Teilhard may even have thought that the very persistence of that gap might be a fruitful and healthy thing.

Those three proposals may occasion some surprise, and I shall try to allay that surprise in a moment. But before attending to that, let me finish with the issue my Reader's univocal use of the term "scientific" raises about this study. It should be clear, first of all, that Teilhard himself consciously intended that term to apply to "hyperphysics" in a radically *different* sense from its legitimate application to any one of the conventional sciences. Hence, what recent philosophers of science may have to say, presumably about sciences in the conventional sense, will not apply to his hyperphysics except in an indirect way. But more than that, if the three proposals made above have any validity, Teilhard would seem to have foreseen that these two senses of "scientific" would, and perhaps should, never merge into one.

The evidence Teilhard's writings furnish for those three proposals is, I have already indicated, no more than fragmentary and allusive. But the plausibility of those proposals should not create insurmountable difficulties; they are,

I submit, entirely coherent with the thought processes which gave birth to his hyperphysics in the first place. His lack of concern, first of all, for how the conventional sciences might change with respect to methods and canons of evidence is simply a matter of record, or absence of it if you prefer. As long as one admits the legitimacy of a hyperphysical interpretation of the conclusions to which any conventional science came, and a hyperphysical coordination of the varied findings of the various conventional sciences, that lack of concern on his part is easily understood.

But, secondly—and here the evidence, though scattered, is more positive—Teilhard makes occasional allusions to the reliability of findings gleaned by the conventional sciences working along the lines of their accepted methodologies and canons of evidence;[5] those allusions lead me to believe that he envisaged that reliability as furnishing the conventional sciences with valid identity papers and approved passports into the future. For once the conventional sciences do their job, one could judge with considerable confidence exactly *what* they had accomplished by bearing in mind just *how* they had set about accomplishing it. Alert to their procedures, and to both the power and the limitations which their procedures entailed, the hyperphysicist could decipher *through* their reported findings the "imposed factors" of the real which they were, each in its specialized language, reporting. The gap between "the sciences" and this "hyper-science" would always remain, but since the features of the multi-leveled evolving real can frequently be got at, and sometimes be got at best, through scientific procedures—and Teilhard "believed in science" to that extent—the gap would always remain a fruitful one: as long, that is, as the hyperphysicist could remain

[5] See, for example, VP 97–98/134–37 on the necessity and advantages of the "analytic" procedures he associates with the more conventional practice of science; the same viewpoint is implied in SC 24–26/50–52 and PM 50, 84, 103/45–46, 84–85, 103: he must first *accept* and respect such analytic findings before he can proceed to "read" them hyperphysically.

sure of how each of the conventional sciences was actually doing its specialized job.[6]

That distinction betwen the two meanings of "scientific," however, also supplies something of a reply to two further strictures Reader suggested might be laid upon me: I had not, he observes, either taken my cue from, or referred to, recent developments either in "evolutionary theory" or in the "philosophy of science." Clearly, both these animadversions would have considerable point if the Teilhardian hyperphysics I meant to explain purported to be "scientific" in the conventional sense of that term. Then it would have been directly incumbent on me to compare it with the—presumably "scientific"—theories of evolution, and to evaluate it in the light of what current philosophers of science have to say about—presumably conventional—science.

The one such comparison I made in these pages, with the views proposed by Jacques Monod, was prompted—apart from his explicit deprecation of Teilhard—by Monod's ambition to construct a "unitary science" to rival and eclipse Teilhard's; the issue there directly bore on the possibilities and problems involved in any such unitary science of the entire evolving real. But reading Monod convinces me that I am far from being the expert in genetic theory required to execute the comparison Reader asks of me. Someone like Theodosius Dobzhansky could do that job much better: but for all his sympathy with Teilhard's overall synthesis, I have been led to question whether even Dobzhansky ever took the exact measure of what Teilhard was about, and how he went about elaborating his hyperphysi-

---

[6] One might be tempted to think Teilhard would have been sympathetic with Paul Feyerabend's tirades *Against Method* (London: NLB; Atlantic Highlands, N.J., Humanities Press, 1975), but I rather suspect the opposite. From the moment one can no longer be sure of what the scientist is doing and how he is doing it, the subsequent task of hyperphysical interpretation becomes risky at best, and, at worst, impossible.

cal vision of our evolutionary past. How would a geneticist evaluate that vision, once its lines were clearly understood? An interesting question, that, and one for an expert geneticist to answer; but he would first have to be alert to the demands involved in comparing the "findings" of conventional genetic theory with the "imposed factors" of the real which Teilhard, in his unconventional way, strove to bring to the surface in order to be "seen." But this, in turn, would require the geneticist's bringing to his task a sensitive awareness of other sciences besides genetics, and some appreciation of their interrelationships. Unable to make that comparison myself, I have limited my task to illuminating the ground rules any such comparison would have to observe—modest progress, Reader might reply, but progress nonetheless.

Nor can I produce impressive credentials in the philosophy of science; my limited conversance with that field is just extensive enough to make me alternate between profound admiration and heartfelt sympathy for those hacking their courageous way through its thickets and tangles in these our times. And yet, I cannot but think that the journeyman's acquaintance I have of the philosophy of science may represent certain advantages for the readers of this work. For had I "taken my cue," in Reader's terms, from recent developments in that field, they might have introduced a factor of "contamination" by anachronism into the readings I have tried to present of these two men, Duhem and Teilhard. Witness the shoddy misreadings of Teilhard from people who claimed to know something of the philosophy of science, and who allowed their preoccupations to screen them from seeing with fresh eyes what was actually being said. If the cautionary tale unfolded in these pages has one moral, it is clearly this: when claiming they were reading Teilhard, philosophers of science have seldom distinguished themselves by the conscientious homework they brought to that task. I think of this book as pointing out to them where they have further homework to do rather than as doing it for them.

And yet, even from my rudimentary knowledge of the philosophy of science, I shall risk some observations farther on. Before I do that, however, let me answer Reader's two last strictures on the book he read: that I failed to refer to any "Teilhard studies" published more recently than some twenty years ago, and, further, that I was obviously using "hermeneutical method," and, indeed, presenting such a hermeneutics of Teilhard's own "hermeneutical method of scientific inquiry" that I owed it to my readers to "display this term prominently" in advising them of what I was doing.

Now, there is only partial justice in the former accusation,[7] but I had thought to have anticipated any such objection in my Introduction: having scoured Teilhardian bibliographies to find some indication which might bear on the precise approach to his method which my personal research had commended to me, I found the cupboard surprisingly bare. No one, so far as I was able to discover, had a word to say about the connection with Pierre Duhem which I (and Reader's remarks of positive appreciation imply that he agrees) found such a fruitful key for understanding Teilhard's developing thought on this precise issue. This may be a comment on the general quality of Teilhardian scholarship, or it is conceivable that I may have missed out on something hidden away somewhere; all I can say is that I looked, looked carefully, and referred to everything, whether recent or not, which bore directly on the issue which concerned me.

---

[7] Not to press Reader's "twenty-year" hyperbole too hard, but the English edition of VP dates only from 1966, d'Ouince (*Un Prophète en procès*) wrote in 1970, de Lubac (*Lettres intimes*) in 1974; while both McCarthy's bibliography (*Pierre Teilhard de Chardin: A Comprehensive Bibliography*) and King's (highly relevant) study of "knowing" in Teilhard (*Teilhard's Mysticism of Knowing*) date from 1981. See Introduction and notes passim.

But then, this lonely effort to trace the origins and growth of Teilhard's thought out of his early acquaintance with Duhem was, after all, a "hermeneutic" venture. I must confess this charge leaves me nonplused, even a bit bemused. It makes me feel like some latter-day Bourgeois Gentilhomme suddenly accorded the stirring revelation that he has been speaking prose all these years and never realized it. Hermeneutics, indeed; one cannot ply the philosopher's trade without having come across the products of this most recent in philosophy's eternally undiscourageable and equally incorrigible search for some latest Rosetta Stone, *The Method* which will make all future quests for method unnecessary. But to Reader's indictment, however kindly meant, I can only plead innocent; such dark arts I have never consciously practiced, and the thought of crowning this modest effort with so solemn-sounding an accolade makes me dream of scurrying back to my native Astoria to end my days a hermit there.

What I have done here, despite occasional intricacies, is a relatively simple thing: I have read what two men wrote, stumbled luckily on a promising connection between them, and then gone carefully about re-reading them to test whether the promise held a pay-off. That process of careful reading and re-reading persuaded me that both men have often been misread, and I have merely tried to coach the interested reader on how he or she might approach their writings in order to test my own interpretation of them.

But both men continue to be misread. I have tried to show this of Teilhard—but "serious" philosophers of science, content that the earlier verdict of their peers rightfully banished him to the outer darkness in store for those who do not merit serious attention, no longer read him at all. Duhem, however, is quite a different matter: having long ignored him, philosophers of science have come more recently to realize they can ignore him no longer.

I shall limit my survey of recent appreciations of Duhem's work to those areas of his achievement which have special relevance to Teilhard's hyperphysical synthesis. The first of those areas to beckon for renewed attention was his proposal that any physical theory had to be judged as a totality, and could not be judged on any other terms. The older, "received view"[8] of scientific method was just beginning to be challenged when Willard Van Orman Quine resurrected, and strongly argued for, what is currently being termed the Duhem–Quine "network view" of scientific theory.[9] What seems to have caught the primary attention of more recent thinkers is the corollary of that network view: that no single observation which appeared to falsify some element in a theory could really be held to falsify it, after all. The *experimentum crucis* was really a myth, since it cannot be determined, logically, which particular facet of the total theory really comes under attack; adjustments can be made to any number of other facets in order to take the presumed counter-verification into account, and so square the theory with the results of observation. It would not do, it was subsequently argued,[10] to appeal to the distinction, widely held in the received view, between "theoretical" and "observational" statements, for Duhem's intuition, here as well, was basically sound: every

[8] For good characterizations of the "received" view, see John P. Losee's *A Historical Introduction to the Philosophy of Science* (London & New York: Oxford University Press, 1972; repr. 1980), pp. 173–202, and more analytically, *The Structure of Scientific Theories*, ed. Frederick Suppe (Urbana: University of Illinois Press, 1974), esp. pp. 6–61.

[9] See Quine's essay on "Two Dogmas of Empiricism" in his *From a Logical Point of View: Nine Logico-Philosophical Essays* (Cambridge: Harvard University Press, 1954; repr. New York: Harper & Row, 1963).

[10] The contemporary writer best known for exploiting Duhem's ideas is Mary B. Hesse. See, on the precise issue here, her "Is There an Independent Observation Language?" in *The Nature and Function of Scientific Theories: Essays in Contemporary Science and Philosophy*, ed. Robert G. Colodny (Pittsburgh: University of Pittsburgh Press, 1970), pp. 35–77; as well as her *The Structure of Scientific Inference* (Berkeley: University of California Press, 1974), pp. 2–5, 24–27, and her earlier *Models and Analogies in Science* (Notre Dame, Ind.: University of Notre Dame Press, 1966), esp. pp. 1–5.

observation statement, in physics at least, was already to some extent theory-laden. This one of Duhem's fundamental contentions, therefore, equally fundamental to Teilhard's project, is both alive and kicking in the contemporary literature.

A second of Duhem's major propositions, however, seems to have provoked a series of misunderstandings. He argued that no physical theory which claimed to be genuinely scientific could simultaneously claim to be "explanatory" of the physical reality whose "laws" (much closer to the level of observation) it aimed to coordinate and unify. This proposition seems to have disquieted certain writers on science[11] dedicated to the belief that physical theory does indeed tell us something about observable reality even if, as they will admit, what it is telling us requires sagacious and sometimes sophisticated decoding. To give the philosopher of science an additional homework assignment, I suggest that Duhem has not been correctly understood; the kind of "explanation" he meant to exclude from physical theory is explicitly designated as "metaphysical." His principal adversary in this connection was mechanism, and the illustration of his contention takes the form of probing historical examples of physical syntheses, whether Gassendi's, Newton's, or Huygens', which claimed to derive their power to "represent" physical reality, with scientific correctness, from the metaphysical view that physical reality is mechanistic, and deterministic, in its inner nature and profoundest workings.[12] That claim, Duhem strove to show, did not bear up under close examination; in every case where the claim was made, it could be shown

---

[11] See Leonard K. Nash, *The Nature of the Natural Sciences* (Boston: Little, Brown, 1963), esp. pp. 241–42; but compare the different slant of his remarks on Duhem's notion of "natural classification" (p. 371).

[12] The derivation could be deductive, inductive, or a mixture of both; the point Duhem is attacking is the necessary entailment between scientific theory and metaphysical explanation, however that entailment is argued for.

that the "representative" value of the theory on the scientific level was entirely independent of the "explanatory" value its author claimed for the mechanistic metaphysics he espoused.

How, then, is one to judge whether one physical theory is a more adequate "representation" than its rivals? We have seen Duhem's answer to this: one makes that judgment in terms of which theory approaches more nearly to the ideal of all scientific theory, a "natural classification." But the status of that affirmation, that the ideal of any total theory is to approach (asymptotically, obviously[13]) a natural classification, Duhem points out, is a peculiar one: it is at one and the same time inscribed as implicit in all the examples of scientific theorizing which history offers for our inspection, and yet is, paradoxically, an affirmation which transcends the methodological canons to which the scientist as scientist is obliged to subscribe. In short, it is an affirmation of another order, whether one call it epistemological or metaphysical; the scientist cannot justify it scientifically, and yet he must implicitly subscribe to it if his continued application to the business of science is to make any reality claims whatever.

Duhem claimed to have refuted the proposition that the successful pursuit of physical science depended on the prior acceptance of a mechanistic metaphysics; that claim earned him the now-famous soubriquet coined by Abel Rey: he was proposing for general acceptance the "physics of a believer."[14] We have seen how Stephen Toulmin quotes, in a manner misleading at very least, the title of the essay which Duhem wrote in reply to that charge. But Toulmin is far from being the only contemporary to imply that Duhem's theorizing was a thinly veiled "apologetics" for a Thomist–Aristotelian metaphysic and, the implication tac-

---

[13] See note 11, above.

[14] See Duhem's account in the essay bearing this title; it is printed as an Appendix in the second edition of his work and in *Aim and Structure*, trans. Wiener, pp. 271–311.

itly runs, for Christianity.[15] Once put into print, of course, such convenient put-downs need only be repeated often enough to become accepted dogma, "so ready," Duhem puts it, "is the human mind to believe what it wishes."[16]

The fair-minded reader can do no better than to return to that essay of Duhem's, and judge the matter for himself. Duhem presents a sketch of his own development from his earlier *acceptance* of mechanism—still embraced, he notes, by some of his fellow-believing Catholics—through the various stages which brought him, purely from the exigencies imposed by an adequate understanding of what sound physical theory implied, to his final position. But interwoven with that autobiographical account, he presents a tightly woven summary of his philosophy of physics which is a masterpiece of condensation and exactitude.

But, even the fair-minded reader would have to object, Duhem does, in fact, end up by commending the Aristotelian view of the material world as his preferred "metaphysic," his preferred philosophical cosmology. Has he fallen into the very trap Abel Rey had set for him, and revealed himself as the "apologist" that even later thinkers claim he was, or must have been, all along?

To answer that charge—so like the ones later leveled against Teilhard—one must follow carefully the steps which led Duhem to commend Aristotelianism in the precise way he came to commend it. That care, I suggest, may turn out to be more rewarding than initially appears; not only will it inform any judgment about Duhem's guilt or innocence as an "apologist," but it may suggest, as well, avenues of reflection on the reality value of scientific theorizing which are surprisingly relevant to contemporary concerns.

What, then, led Duhem to commend the Aristotelian

[15] See, for example, Nash, *Nature of the Natural Sciences*, p. 357; how this charge coheres with Nash's other observations about Duhem I am unable to see.

[16] *Aim and Structure*, trans. Wiener, p. 275.

cosmology? It was, he assures us, his study of physical theories as history presents them to us, a study which he was later to encase, albeit incompletely, in his historical survey of "World Systems." That work represents an analytic history of science both guided by and reinforcing his original conviction that science has always sought, and to remain scientific must continue to seek, as its "ideal form," its culminating fulfillment, the "natural classification" of observable reality. But can one, on the basis of such an analytic history of science, be bold enough to project the shape such an eventual "natural classification" might assume? Yes, Duhem replies, to some extent at least: and then he proceeds to sketch, on purely scientific grounds, the general shape that classification would have to take.

But even if one take this dare, the natural classification one projects would still remain on the scientific level, and never, on Duhem's own principles, rise (or deepen) to the "metaphysical" or "cosmological" level occupied by the Aristotelian synthesis. Not only does Duhem admit this, he proclaims it. On what grounds, then, can he conclude to his commendation of Aristotelianism?

Clearly not, Duhem was convinced, on the grounds claimed by his mechanistic adversaries, who thought that the "explanatory" power of their scientific theories could be derived, in some semi-deductive way, from the metaphysic they envisioned as intimately mated to them. No, Duhem proposes, the relationship between the ideal natural classification which the progressive history of science adumbrates, and the metaphysical cosmology toward which he was personally convinced it pointed, must be a relationship of "analogy," neither more nor less than that.

At this juncture in his argument, however, Duhem frankly warns his readers that he has left the domain of science, and entered the domain of metaphysics. Inconsistent with his prior claims, this sudden avowal? Not in the least. His claim has been, from the very first, that the scientist's mute aspiration toward a natural classification embodied a commitment the scientist could never in practice contravene, but at the same time could never, on scientific grounds, either justify or fully explain.

It should be noticed, though, that now there are two analogical gaps which Duhem's construction obliges us to bridge. The first of them stretches—horizontally—between the actual form any concrete historical theory assumes and the "natural classificatory" theory which the progressive history of science prompts the mind to project. The second stretches—vertically—between that ideal theory and the metaphysical cosmology with which it most closely corresponds.

How is the mind to bridge these gaps? For choosing between false and genuine analogies is a notoriously slippery business, in which individual subjectivity can play a dangerous role. Duhem is keenly aware of those dangers, but such choices are constantly being made in the practice of science itself; indeed, the practice of science can be viewed as an excellent school for the education of that "good sense" which equips the skillful scientist with the power of judgment required in these matters. For that, when all is said, is the key term: sound judgment.

This is the point where Duhem's analysis of the history of science intersects with another stream of contemporary concern among philosophers of science. For Quine's revival of the network view of theory was scarcely the last shot fired against the received view. Paul Feyerabend had long been spraying the ramparts with a series of criticisms which culminated in the "anarchistic" proposal—Feyerabend's own term—spelled out in his book *Against Method*.[17] But now a distinguished scientist, Michael Polanyi, climaxed his own criticisms of the regnant view and its quest for a purely "objective" knowledge of the observable real. No scientist, he claimed, ever got anywhere that way: science

[17] See above, note 6.

is, always has been, and must be an affair of *Personal Knowledge*.[18] Subjectivity, personal judgment, is ineradicably and indispensably woven into the process whereby the ongoing community of scientific knowers, down through human history, arrives at its agreements on what constitutes good science and sound scientific findings. The "authority" of science reposes, then, not in some impersonal set of "rules," some canonized type of scientific "method" valid for all times and all places; the authority which any scientific finding eventually gains arises from the persons constituting the scientific community, each and all exercising their mutually corrective, and ultimately reinforcing, judgments.

But surely the watershed work of recent times was Thomas S. Kuhn's historical analysis of *The Structure of Scientific Revolutions*, first published in 1962.[19] It reads in ways like a companion piece to Polanyi's less historically anchored argument. Kuhn sees scientists of any particular epoch practicing their trade in terms of one or other accepted "paradigm"—a troublesome term, as Kuhn was later to acknowledge.[20] He further claims that science has progressed, not always in the more gradualistic and cumulative manner which the formerly received theory would call for, but often by revolutionary jumps, each featuring the overthrow of one entire paradigm and its replacement, with the suddenness of a "gestalt switch," by a new one, largely incommensurable with the older. But how do these jumps occur? Again, Kuhn proposes that a new paradigm gains acceptance principally because the scientific com-

18 See chap. 3, note 6.
19 See chap. 1, note 16.
20 For a valuable summary of the controversy Kuhn's work inspired, see *Paradigms and Revolutions*, ed. Gary Gutting (Notre Dame, Ind.: University of Notre Dame Press, 1980), esp. the editor's Introduction, pp. 1–21. Gutting is perhaps more sympathetic to Kuhn than others might be, but the history he presents of the question is trustworthy in the main.

munity at any one time comes to place its "authority" behind it.

No sooner had Kuhn's suggestions seen the light of day than a swarm of objectors flew at him from every side.[21] Hardly a paragraph he had penned escaped attack, but at the heart of all the resulting cacophony one note sounded repetitive and clear: his proposals were tantamount to replacing the revered ideal of impersonal objectivity with the anarchy of subjectivity which Feyerabend also seemed to be advocating. Claiming that the authority of science reposed in the communities of scientists which succeed each other over the centuries was equivalent to stripping science of any legitimate authority whatever. Or, put another way: the discipline formerly known as the philosophy of science would now, in the extreme case at least, collapse into the history of science; what was once a quest for rules, norms, or standards for legitimate scientific procedure could now turn into a dreary record of the different ways in which different scientists have in fact gone about the business they were pleased to denominate as "scientific." If Kuhn is correct, his critics concluded, science is little more than what scientists actually do, and no one has more or less right to call himself a scientist than anyone else! Another night has come in which all cows are black and indistinguishable from one another.

The modifications Kuhn was later brought to introduce into his proposal need not directly concern us here. More relevant is Larry Laudan's brilliant attempt[22] to show how the philosophy of science could profit from the history of science, but the history of science itself be written in the light of that quest for standards of "rationality," legitimate acceptability, which the philosophy of science has always

---

[21] See the bibliography in ibid., pp. 321–39.

[22] See especially his *Progress and Its Problems: Toward a Theory of Scientific Growth* (Berkeley: University of California Press, 1977).

cherished: cherished, but often in some timeless world of logical abstractions which could, and sometimes did, display only the remotest relevance to how scientists actually do science.

But Laudan's project commits him to making a selection of certain "standard" examples of what will count as genuinely scientific activity, while bearing in mind the shifting standards of rationality to which the history of human intelligence bears witness. And once again, the need for what Duhem called "good judgment" is manifest. Indeed, it has been argued[23] that a generous interpretation of both Kuhn and Polanyi leaves us with three basic insights as their central and solid contribution to the ongoing debate: that the task of making judgments is the burden every reflective person must inescapably bear; that no unambiguous set of "rules" exists to assure us infallibly when the soundest possible judgment has been felled in any given case; and finally, perhaps most crucially, that the subjectivity, the personal ingredient which enters into any process of judgment, need not be deemed the antithesis of "objectivity"— a properly educated subjectivity is, in fact, one of the indispensable requirements for good judgments on how things objectively stand.

Kuhn has replied to his critics that the history of science must be read with certain "values" in mind. That term "values" seems to raise in the minds of certain thinkers the specter of rampant subjectivity again; so, Laudan's suggestion expresses it, we must propose a set of concrete "exemplars" of what would be universally accepted as "scientific" achievement in the genuine sense, and then compare other, more ambiguous cases, with those exemplars. For

23 Most notably by Gutting; see note 20, above. Laudan, *Progress and Its Problems,* pp. 72–78, 141–43, 206–207, 215–16, and 228–34, is more generally negative, but not, I submit, in a way which entirely repudiates Gutting's approach or the point about "judgment" which I am making here. For Duhem's repeated appeals to judgment at various levels of the scientific process, see his *Aim and Structure,* trans. Wiener, pp. 163, 171, 216–17, 290ff.

while exemplars embody values, they also manifest noetic contours as well, contours which can be "gotten at," within limits at least.

This entire debate, I suggest, has brought contemporary thinkers round to a position startlingly like the one Duhem already occupied some eighty years ago. To learn what constitutes genuine scientific activity, he wrote then, one cannot ignore the history of science; and yet, one must be able to read the history of science with some normative "ideal" in view, all the time aware that the ideal may never have been completely realized in any single historical instance. Duhem expressed that normative ideal in his term "natural classification," and that notion, I suggest, may well be rediscovered as his network view of theory has been, and prove serviceable today. Indeed, to go a step farther, it is conceivable that Duhem's monumental start on writing a normatively oriented history of science, his *Systèmes du monde*, might merit a long second, or, in the case of many workers in the field, a fresh and unprejudiced first, look. It could well furnish fruitful indications of what the "exemplar" of Laudan's philosophical history of science might resemble.[24]

Any fresh appreciation of Duhem, however, is bound to bring in its wake some dawning realization that Teilhard's attempt to construct a "vision of the past" may merit, in its turn, fresh evaluation. Nourished by Duhem's philosophical view of science as a progressive historical human enterprise, Teilhard sought to flesh out the ideal of "natural

[24] I would suggest to the judgment of more competent students in this field that the other points of contact between Laudan's presentation and (less noticed features of) Duhem's thought would repay careful examination. Chief among them would be Laudan's discussion of the empirical–conceptual mix involved in the progress of science (*Progress and Its Problems*, pp. 66–69; compare p. 230*n*11); the frequent ingredredience of non-scientific considerations in any "research tradition," along with the possibility of filtering out the strictly scientific elements of any such tradition (pp. 79–94, pp. 82–86 and 94 being of special interest); and the "truth value" or lack of it in scientific theories (pp. 125–27).

classification" which presided over Duhem's efforts. I have deliberately saved his name until now, but it is remarkable that one of the earlier critics of the prevailing notion of science as a kind of timeless pursuit undergoing no significant historical transformations was Stephen Toulmin: his view of science as itself an "evolving" reality[25] may well have sensitized him to Teilhard's repeated claim that he was engaged in doing science as it might be done in the future. It may have been an equally careless reading of Duhem's achievement which resulted in Toulmin's failure to recognize the Duhemian heritage which fed bone and sinew into Teilhard's way of reconstructing humanity's evolutionary past. But then, one pays close attention to those one has already decided are worth that attention; having dismissed Duhem as an "apologist," it may have been a reflex action for him to dismiss Teilhard equally out of hand. There are, however, striking kinship features between the evolutionary views of scientific development which both men shared, and no small irony in the one's insensitivity to what his opposite number was really about.

A final reminder, however: Teilhard's endeavor to elaborate a "natural classification" of the observable real, while taking its initial inspiration from Duhem, was the farthest thing from a slavish schoolboy imitation. In the course of explaining that notion, Duhem argued for extending the accepted boundaries defining "physics" in his day; and yet, even with those extended boundaries, his proposal remained recognizable as a "physics," and his ideal physics very close to a science in the conventional sense. By extending Duhem's insight across the entire spectrum of the observable real, however, Teilhard brought the notion of natural classification to another level of discourse: to a "scientific" level, but a level where science bears only an

[25] See especially his *Foresight and Understanding: An Inquiry into the Aims of Science* (Bloomington: Indiana University Press, 1961; repr. New York: Harper & Row, 1963), where he propounds this view of scientific activity and progress.

analogous relationship to science in its conventionally accepted sense. By so doing, he confronts us with a third analogy-gap to deal with: whereas Duhem compels us to judge on the analogy between physics and its ideal form, and then on the analogy between that ideal form and its corresponding cosmology, Teilhard intercalates his "hyperphysics" at an intermediary level, between the ideal type of any single science—be it physics, biology, sociology, or whatever—and the metaphysical cosmology he may have thought most closely corresponded to this unitary view of the entire evolving universe.

When constructing that vision of the past, moreover, Teilhard seldom engages in those highly technical discussions which rightly preoccupy philosophers of science; he seldom answers our queries to supply a list of "rules" for the conduct of his enterprise. He simply goes about his hyperphysical business, discerning his "imposed factors," constantly making judgments of analogy between the levels of science and their corresponding levels of the real, trusting that our educated subjectivity will find those judgments sound. He seems to have been more anxious to leave behind, in Laudan's term, an "exemplar" of how it might be done, while leaving to lesser mortals like myself the task of gathering up what fragmentary clues he left and fitting them together in an explanation of how he went about his task.[26]

But the implicit philosophy of conventional science Teilhard brought to his construction is Duhem's at so many crucial turnings that whatever the future may judge of the one, it may be called upon to render a comparable judgment on the other. For they both were arguing against

---

[26] Laudan's criteria (*Progress and Its Problems*, pp. 178–80) would probably classify my work in these pages as "exegesis" rather than "explanation"; but explanation cannot be sound except when solidly based on the results of careful exegesis. It is wisest to go step by step in these matters, and not to invite some prematurely formed explanation to contaminate the results of the prior exegetical stage; compare my remarks above, pp. 179–80 of this chapter.

views and myths of science which are currently under withering bombardment; and both reminded us that science was an historical reality rather than some unchanging pursuit whose inflexible rules had been clearly established once and for all. For both, the conception of a scientific "revolution," resulting in that temporary dialogue of deaf men which Kuhn describes, was a genuine possibility; for both, an analytic history of science could confidently ground the judgment that science, while always remaining provisional in its findings, was nonetheless progressive in its movement, a movement toward "natural classification."

Both of them claimed, further, that when the physicist, seduced by the allure of mathematical exactitude which characterized his theories, concluded that reality itself must be mechanistic and deterministic in nature, he was maladroitly playing the metaphysician unawares; that physics could not legitimately be taken as a model for its other sister sciences, but that there may nonetheless be some principle of analogous unity which bound the whole array of sciences together—a principle which required recognizing the respective claims of experimental and experiential knowledge, and bringing those claims into a healthy working relationship. Both Duhem and Teilhard, after him, recognized that no scientific "fact" was ever pure atomic fact, but observed reality already drenched in viewpoint, interest, theory; that any total theory must be judged as such, in terms of its coherence, self-consistency, *and* its ability to classify, "naturally," whatever total realm of observables it assumed into its purview; that any such judgment required, not the elimination, but the education, of the subjectivity which unavoidably enters into the judging process—in short, that some people, scientists or not, can simply "see" better than others.[27]

[27] For the encouragement Teilhard might plausibly have found in Duhem for these additional insights, see Duhem's *Aim and Structure*, trans. Wiener, pp. 160, 177, 211–12, 216–17 (on scientific revolutions); pp. 180–83 (on physics

Recent developments in the philosophy of science have created a far more "open" atmosphere, in which this entire litany of Duhemian–Teilhardian propositions seems far more acceptable than to scientists of thirty, or even twenty, years ago. That new openness might soon encourage a fresh, untrammeled examination of the exemplar Teilhard has left us. There may be far more here for our instruction than our blinkered eyes of yesteryear could make out.

---

and its relation to the other sciences); pp. 158–59, 163, 166–67, 178–79, and 259–68 (on experimental and experiential knowledge); and pp. 163, 171, 190–98, and 216–17 (on the subjective input into scientific judgments). But whether derived from Duhem or arrived at independently, these are crucial points on which Teilhard's agreements with Duhem suggest that a judgment made about the one will be linked with a comparable judgment on the achievement of the other.

Bibliography

Armagnac, Christian d'. "Philosophie de la nature et méthode chez le Père Teilhard de Chardin." *Archives de Philosophie*, 20, No. 1 (January–March 1957), 4–41.

Barbour, George B. *In the Field with Teilhard de Chardin.* New York: Herder & Herder, 1965.

Barthélémy-Madaule, Madeleine. *La Personne et le drame humain chez Teilhard de Chardin.* Paris: Editions du Seuil, 1967.

Capra, Fritjof. *The Tao of Physics: An Exploration of the Parallels Between Modern Physics and Eastern Mysticism.* Berkeley: Shambala, 1975.

Cuénot, Claude. *Teilhard de Chardin: A Biographical Study.* Trans. Vincent Colimore. Ed. René Hague. Baltimore: Helicon, 1965.

Dobzhansky, Theodosius. *The Biology of Ultimate Concern.* New York: World, 1969.

——. *Mankind Evolving.* New Haven: Yale University Press, 1962.

——. "Pierre Teilhard de Chardin as a Scientist." In Teilhard de Chardin, *Letters to Two Friends, 1926–1952.* New York: New American Library, 1968. Pp. 219–27.

Duhem, Pierre. *The Aim and Structure of Physical Theory.* Trans. Philip P. Wiener. Princeton: Princeton University Press, 1954. Repr. New York: Atheneum, 1962.

——. "La Théorie physique: Son Objet, sa structure." *Revue de Philosophie*, 4–6 (April 1904–June 1905). Thirteen articles.

Feyerabend, Paul. *Against Method.* London: NLB; Atlantic Highlands, N.J.: Humanities Press, 1975.

Hesse, Mary B. "Is There an Independent Observation Language?" In *The Nature and Function of Scientific Theories:*

Essays in Contemporary Science and Philosophy. Ed. Robert G. Colodny. Pittsburgh: University of Pittsburgh Press, 1970. Pp. 35–77.

——. *Models and Analogies in Science.* Notre Dame, Ind.: University of Notre Dame Press, 1966.

——. *The Structure of Scientific Inference.* Berkeley: University of California Press, 1974.

King, Thomas. *Teilhard's Mysticism of Knowing.* New York: Seabury, 1981.

Kuhn, Thomas S. *The Structure of Scientific Revolutions.* Chicago: The University of Chicago Press, 1962. 2nd rev. ed.: 1970.

Laudan, Larry. *Progress and Its Problems.* Berkeley: University of California Press, 1977.

Losee, John P. *A Historical Introduction to the Philosophy of Science.* London & New York: Oxford University Press, 1972. Repr. 1980.

Lubac, Henri de, s.j. *The Religion of Teilhard de Chardin.* Trans. René Hague. New York: Desclée, 1967.

Lukas, Mary. "Teilhard and the Piltdown 'Hoax.'" *America,* 144, No. 20 (May 23, 1981), 424–27.

Manquat, M. "Une Critique du transformisme." *Revue des Questions Scientifiques,* 85, No. 2 (April 1924), 370–87.

McCarthy, Joseph M. *Pierre Teilhard de Chardin: A Comprehensive Bibliography.* New York & London: Garland, 1981.

Medawar, P. B. Review of Teilhard de Chardin, *The Phenomenon of Man.* In *Mind,* 70, No. 277 (January 1961), 99–106.

Monod, Jacques. *Chance and Necessity: An Essay on the Natural Philosophy of Modern Biology.* Trans. Austryn Wainhouse. New York: Knopf, 1971.

Nash, Leonard K. *The Nature of the Natural Sciences.* Boston: Little, Brown, 1963.

O'Connell, Robert J., s.j. Review of Thomas King, *Teilhard's Mysticism of Knowing.* In *Theological Studies,* 43, No. 1 (March 1982), 160–62.

Ouince, René d'. *Un Prophète en procès.* 2 vols. Paris: Aubier–Montaigne, 1970.

Pantin, Carl. *The Relations Between the Sciences.* Cambridge: Cambridge University Press, 1968.

Paradigms and Revolutions. Ed. Gary Gutting. Notre Dame, Ind.: University of Notre Dame Press, 1980.

Polanyi, Michael. *Personal Knowledge: Towards a Post-Critical Philosophy.* Chicago: The University of Chicago Press, 1958. Corrected ed.: 1962.

———. *The Tacit Dimension.* Garden City, N.Y.: Doubleday, 1966.

Polgár, László, S.J. *Internationale Teilhard-Bibliographie, 1955–1965.* Freiburg & Munich: Alber, 1965.

Quine, Willard Van Orman. *From a Logical Point of View: Nine Logico-Philosophical Essays.* Cambridge: Harvard University Press, 1954. Repr. New York: Harper & Row, 1963.

Rabut, Olivier, O.P. *Teilhard de Chardin: A Critical Study.* New York: Sheed & Ward, 1961.

Rousselot, Pierre, S.J. "Les Yeux de la foi," *Recherches des Sciences Religieuses*, 1 (1910), 241–59.

Simpson, George Gaylord. Review of Teilhard de Chardin, *The Phenomenon of Man.* In *Scientific American*, 202, No. 4 (April 1960), 201–207.

Skinner, B. F. *Beyond Freedom and Dignity.* New York: Knopf, 1971.

The Structure of Scientific Theories. Ed. Frederick Suppe. Urbana: University of Illinois Press, 1974.

Terra, Helmut de. *Memories of Teilhard de Chardin.* Trans. J. Maxwell Brownjohn. New York: Harper & Row, 1964.

Toulmin, Stephen. *Foresight and Understanding: An Inquiry into the Aims of Science.* Bloomington: Indiana University Press, 1961. Repr. New York: Harper & Row, 1963.

———. "On Teilhard de Chardin." *Commentary*, 39, No. 3 (March 1965), 50–55.

Vialleton, Louis. *Membres et ceintures des vertébrés tétrapodes: Critique morphologique du transformisme.* Paris: Doin, 1924.

Zukav, Gary. *The Dancing Wu Li Masters: An Overview of the New Physics.* New York: Morrow, 1979.

TEILHARD DE CHARDIN, Pierre, S.J.

The Appearance of Man. Trans. J. M. Cohen. New York: Harper & Row, 1965.

"De l'Arbitraire dan les lois, théories, et principes de la physique." *Quodlibeta,* 2 (1905), 247–74.

The Future of Man. Trans. Norman Denny. New York: Harper & Row, 1964.

The Heart of Matter. Trans. René Hague. New York: Harcourt, Brace, Jovanovich, 1979.

Human Energy. Trans. J. M. Cohen. New York: Harcourt, Brace, Jovanovich, 1971.

Letters from a Traveller. London: Collins, 1962.

Letters to Two Friends, 1926–1952. New York: New American Library, 1968.

Lettres intimes à Auguste Valensin, Bruno de Solages, Henri de Lubac, André Ravier, 1919–1955. Ed. Henri de Lubac, S.J. Paris: Aubier–Montaigne, 1974.

The Making of a Mind: Letters from a Soldier–Priest, 1914–1919. Trans. René Hague. New York: Harper & Row, 1965.

The Phenomenon of Man. Trans. Bernard Wall. New York: Harper & Row, 1959. Rev. ed., 1965.

Science and Christ. Trans. René Hague. New York: Harper & Row, 1968.

The Vision of the Past. Trans. J. M. Cohen. New York: Harper & Row, 1966.

Writings in the Time of War. Trans. René Hague. New York: Harper & Row, 1968.

Index